GEORGE BISHOP
SEVENTEENTH-CENTURY SOLDIER TURNED QUAKER

D1111692

Firgrove, Chew Magna, Bristol. Home of George Bishop's daughter Elizabeth and her husband, Richard Vickris.

The signature of George Bishop on the front cover is the final part of the fascimile letter which appears on page 39. It is Crown copyright, reference SP 23/114, and has been reproduced by courtesy of the Controller of Her Majesty's Stationery Office.

GEORGE BISHOP

SEVENTEENTH-CENTURY SOLDIER
TURNED QUAKER

by

MARYANN S. FEOLA

William Sessions Limited
The Ebor Press
York, England

ISBN 1 85072 178 5

Maryann S. Feola is an Assistant Professor of English at the College of Staten Island, City University of New York. She is Coordinator of the Program in Science, Letters and Society.

Printed in 11/12 point Plantin Typeface
from Author's Disk
by William Sessions Limited
The Ebor Press
York, England

North American Distributors:
Syracuse University Press Inc.
1600 Jamesville Avenue
Syracuse, 13244-5160
New York, USA

TABLE OF CONTENTS

For Stephanie —
Grateful for our friendship
and your devotion! to a free press.
Melton!? Maryann ✗✗ oo
24;; 2017

for my father, Thomas J. Feola
printer emeritus, *New York Times*

Books are not absolutely dead things, but do contain a potency of life in them to be as active as that soul whose progeny they are: no they do preserve as in a vial the purest efficacy and extraction of that living intellect that bred them. I know they are as lively, and as vigorously productive, as those fabulous Dragon's teeth; and being sown up and down, may chance to spring up armed men.

> from *Areopagitica; A Speech of Mr. John Milton for the Liberty of Unlicenc'd Printing. To the Parliament of England. 1644.*

PREFACE

THE ENGLISH QUAKER GEORGE BISHOP (d. 1668) was a leading organizer and publicist in his native Bristol who authored more
than thirty tracts. Committed to securing religious liberty for the
"Children of the Light," he worked closely with early organizers,
including George Fox and Margaret Fell, disseminating Quaker
ideas and seeking to secure the protection of disapproving magistrates and ministers. During the English civil wars, Bishop was a
Parliamentary soldier and civil servant who called for harsh
measures in reckoning with King Charles I. However, during his
final years, he became an advocate of passive resistance in response
to the violence Quakers met because of the Restoration religious
settlement. This book explores Bishop's military and civil service
experiences, as well as his early Quaker writing and organizing
efforts in Bristol until 1660. A subsequent study will examine the
works he wrote during the last eight years of his life and his role in
sustaining the movement in the wake of the laws aimed at noncon-
formists.

     During the intensely religious seventeenth century, the
radicals sought extensive reformation of political and church policies. They envisioned a godly society that would be based on truth
and righteousness. In general they sought liberty of conscience, a
check on the power of the executive and his ministers, and legal
reform. They fought in the civil wars and strove to have their ideas
accepted under the Commonwealth and Protectorate. Yet despite
their efforts, they were disappointed with the policies and practices
of the Cromwellian regime. By illuminating Bishop's disenchantment with political events in Bristol and London, and his subsequent move to Quakerism, we gain added insight into the nature
of the radicals' disillusionment and how sectarian religion became
a valuable repository for their aspirations.

Bishop's extant writing sheds light on what some Quakers-to-be may have initially thought about the execution of the king, the dissolution of the monarchy, and the onslaught of political innovation. A review of his pre-Quaker writing and service to "the Good Old Cause" situates him among those radicals who, according to Christopher Hill, joined the Quakers and other sectarian groups when their political and religious disenchantment became an "experience of defeat."[1] However, unlike most first generation Quakers, Bishop left an illuminating trail of paper that documents specific political events that paved the road to conversion.[2]

This book is a revision of my 1990 City University of New York Ph.D. dissertation. I am grateful to my family, friends, and colleagues who supported me through both stages of this work. James R. Jacob and Stuart Prall deserve special acknowledgment for all those years of advice and encouragement, as do Patrick Cullen and Phyllis Roberts for their suggestions. I am grateful to W. Jerry Frost, who introduced me to George Bishop, and to the late Joseph W. Martin for sharing his views concerning Bishop's work. At different stages of this work, I benefited from discussions with H. Larry Ingle and Michael Mullett. I appreciate the generous assistance from the staff at Friends' Historical Library, Swarthmore College, and from Friends' House Library, London, in particular Malcolm Thomas, Sylvia Carlyle, and Josef Keith. Sheila Walker of Chew Magna, Bristol, deserves a note of thanks for the information and photographs of Firgrove, the home in which Bishop's daughter and her family lived and greeted prominent early Quakers, including William Penn.

While researching this work, I received support from the Office of the Dean of Humanities and Social Sciences, and from the Center for International Service at the College of Staten Island, City University of New York. I also thank Lena Cowen Orlin and her staff at the Folger Shakespeare Institute, Washington, D.C., for the two grants-in-aid that made possible research at the Folger Institute and Library. My participation in their 'Preachers, Petitioners, and Prophets in the Age of Charles I' seminar enriched this work, and I thank Esther Cope, the seminar leader, and my co-participants, especially Byron Nelson, for their feedback on excerpts I presented from it. Like those printers who proved invaluable to the early Quakers, Diane Huntzicker and Barbara Frontera of Flashback Desktop Publishing played a major role in producing this work. Finding their shop the first time helped me "beat the clock" set for a merciless deadline; returning to it six years later was a less frantic but equally rewarding experience. I also thank Barry Sheinkopf for his suggestions and Cynthia Maude-Gembler of Syracuse University Press for her assistance. Like any project this one would not have been completed without input from extraordinary individuals. I am indebted to Dr. Denise Rourke Miller, who helped me negotiate the present so I could better understand the past. My students at the College of Staten Island bring me more energy and inspiration than any other source. My debt to them is tremendous, and they have my heartfelt thanks. Bill Sessions, my publisher, has my gratitude for his astute suggestions and invaluable assistance. Without the generosity I received from him and the trustees of the Sessions Book Trust, I believe that Bishop's story might not have seen the light of publication.

Staten Island, New York

April 1996

NOTES

Throughout this book quotations have been modernized for both spelling and punctuation. During Bishop's lifetime England still followed the older calendar, the new year beginning on 25 March. The dates herein follow the modern Gregorian calendar, the year beginning on 1 January. Consequently, documents originally dated February 1650 now appear as February 1651.

INTRODUCTION

THE INDEPENDENTS, A HETEROGENEOUS group of radicals, emerged in England during the middle decades of the seventeenth century. They grew out of the political and religious opposition that characterized the last decade of Charles I's reign. Their composition challenges definition, as the term "Independents" was used in reference to political and religious groups who frequently differed on a variety of issues. Hence scholars have had difficulty identifying the Independents in Parliament; in the Westminster Assembly of Divines, a body of one hundred and fifty-eight lay and ecclesiastical assessors who were created in 1643 to advise Parliament on church reform; and in the army.

For example, some Independent ministers remained within the Presbyterian church in 1643, perhaps seeing themselves as the reformist flank of the official church.[3] The royalist sympathies of some Independents interested them in the idea of a constitutional monarchy. As would be expected, they objected to any program of drastic reform.[4] More radical Independents, on the other hand, petitioned for social reform and a broader franchise. The Independents, however, agreed that there should be a check on the power of the king and his ministers, and a reformation of the legal system. Most of them favored a decentralized system of congregations, and although they failed to agree on its definition, they advocated liberty of conscience.

Despite the fact that they were on the side that had defeated the king's army in the civil wars, many Independents felt a sense of disillusionment during the period of the Commonwealth and Protectorate. George Bishop was among these disenchanted radical Independents. Hill has commented that Bishop was among the radicals who became sectaries and encountered political disappointment before the 1660 restoration of the king.[5] Bishop appears with some frequency in studies of the period, particularly in those

1

concerning soldiers and civil servants who devoted their enthusiasm to radical religion as they severed their ties with the government. Yet although his contemporaries recognized him as a formidable figure, there has been no full-length study of his military, political, and Quaker activities. One historian suggested that this may be due to Bishop's regicidal and military connections, which preceded his conversion.[6] Given the combination of these earlier comments and the role he assumed as a Quaker organizer and publicist, however, such a study of Bishop will deepen our understanding of the movement's beginning and shed light on the broader picture of England during the civil wars and Interregnum. The experience of George Bishop also illustrates how the shift to sectarian religion became an outlet for the political disenchantment of some radicals. Therefore, this account of the events that resulted in Bishop's joining the Quakers revolves around two questions: first, what were the main and underlying circumstances that caused his disenchantment; and second, to what extent was Bishop's early Quakerism an extension of his radicalism? It is essential to begin with an exploration of the events that shaped the radical Independents.

In England radical groups with political or religious objectives had appeared periodically since time out of memory. Yet they were generally disorganized movements that centered around a charismatic figure, a poor harvest, or some spontaneous source of discontent. In contrast, for a variety of reasons, the radical Independents in the English civil wars were a more sustained force.

Before the war, Puritan pamphleteers including William Prynne, John Bastwick, and Henry Burton frequently criticized the king's court, the Anglican bishops, and the church's Roman-like practices. Their trial in the Court of Star Chamber, and the severe punishment that followed, angered and unified a growing opposition to court policy. It must be remembered that the seventeenth century was a deeply religious time in which church and political issues were virtually indistinguishable. Metaphors of the apocalypse were plentiful; and discontent—that of the king's party and that of their opponents—was expressed in ways that evoked images of a battle between the forces of righteousness and those of evil. In this atmosphere, according to one modern commentator, events such as the ear cropping of Prynne, Bastwick, and Burton served to create martyrs for the opposition's cause.[7]

During the war, soldiers in the New Model Army fought alongside radical preachers like William Dell, Hugh Peter, and John Saltmarsh. Singing as they rode into battle, the preachers reminded the soldiers that, when peace came, they must repay God's providence by restoring honesty and simplicity to the church.[8] Hence, the spiritual fervor of the time, whipped up in the ranks of the New Model Army whence the radical Independents emerged, added a divine stamp of approval to their political and religious visions of reform.

The confusion of authority that the war created also contributed to the radical Independents' emergence. In peacetime the monarchy would have quickly checked the agitation that characterized the units in the New Model Army. Yet during the war, outspoken junior officers were allowed to speak freely, often counseling their superiors. Needing their strength, the army's high command entertained and sometimes embraced the ideas of those who would fight for the liberties they believed Charles I had arrogantly usurped by subordinating fundamental law to the royal prerogative.

The soldiers' demands increased and radicalized, it appears, as the struggle became more complex and victory for Parliament's army became more evident. Parliament's accusations of treason had resulted in the executions of the Archbishop of Canterbury, William Laud, and the king's principal advisor, the Earl of Strafford. It soon became clear that the uncompromising king might share their fate. In this climate of dramatic innovation, those who were discontented with social, religious, political, or military conditions began to freely articulate their versions of truth. For example, in 1647 a group of agitators from Colonel Hewson's regiment forwarded a petition to General Fairfax that addressed military, legal, and Parliamentary affairs.[9] Their decision to propose a program of reform revealed their sense of political self-consciousness. From the mid-1640s onward, army petitions for reform appeared regularly.

The frequency of these petitions was facilitated by a growing press that was subject to a censorship that was "intermittent and rarely effective." According to Nigel Smith, the shift from manuscript to print in the 1640s, and the output of pamphlets forstered the circulation of radical ideas.[10] The Presbyterian minister Thomas Hall referred to the shop of radical printer Giles Calvert as "that forge of the devil from whence so many blasphemous lying, scandalous pamphlets for many years past have spread over the land."[11] The Independent Henry Robinson recognized that the printing press had potential to open up minds and effect change. He saw it as "a unique instrument for the exploration of truth."[12] When all the chains of censorship were removed from the press, as well as from all other outlets of Christian expression, ideas would be endowed with spiritual vitality.[13] In 1637 there had been only twenty presses in London; however, after the 1641 abolition of the Court of Star Chamber, and the subsequent relaxation of the Stationers' Company censorship, output in English publication flourished, causing concern that the huge increase in publication threatened to deplete the supply of paper available in England.[14]

In this environment programs of reform circulated freely among the discontented. Before long, sectaries, members of religious groups whose radical notions derived from mystical and Puritan traditions, were relying on print to communicate their ideas, much as Anglicans, Puritans, and Presbyterians had used the pulpit.[15] The listing in Wing's *Short Title Catalogue* shows a relationship between the religious and political views of the authors and their printers. Writers like Bishop worked exclusively with a handful of printers who specialized in radical tracts. Some radicals, including Richard Overton, sometimes published their own work.

Ideas found in these tracts frequently initiated further agitation. For example, during the October and November 1648 army debates at Putney Church, soldiers, offered by alluding to radical tracts, ways in which the kingdom might be safeguarded from destruction. Bishop referred his listeners to the epistolary tract that the mystic preacher, John Saltmarsh, had written to the Council of War in the previous December. The tract warned the Council that they would need the strength of God to settle the nation, and that strength would only be forthcoming through unity and the abandonment of their petty differences.[16]

By 1649 radical Independency had gained enough strength to effect the execution of the king. A coup designed by Ireton and executed by Colonel Pride placed them in the center of power, from where they could exercise the will of the army's high command. Nevertheless, by January 1649 many Independents felt alienated from their more radical associates, as they found themselves reluctant accomplices to the arrest, trial, and execution of the king.[17]

Thus the combination of well-publicized discontent, civil war, the execution of the king, and the replacement of monarchy with a republic brought the radical Independents to the political arena. From there they would represent various models of political, social, and religious reform. This experience caused them to be viewed as the first group of English radicals to exercise power, and the last who would do so until the Chartist movement in the nineteenth century.[18] Their day, they believed, had arrived. Divine providence had blessed the sword of Oliver Cromwell, and his army had delivered them into the godly Commonwealth they must now transform into the New Jerusalem. The detailed ordinance of 4 January 1645, which restructured the church along Presbyterian lines and replaced the *Book of Common Prayer* with the reformed *Directory for the Public Worship of God,* began the spiritual reformation with which they had been charged.[19]

One can imagine the disappointment of the radical Independents when religious reformation stopped far short of their demands. To their chagrin, the more moderate Independents did little in Parliament to abolish the collection of tithes or payment of wages to a university-trained ministry. Moreover, the Blasphemy Act of 1648, which included the death penalty for a second offense, was directed at radical sectaries, whose eccentric behavior offended most Independents.[20]

The difference in their understanding of liberty of conscience distanced the Independents and the radical sectaries, and was a major cause of the latter group's discontent. This difference is highlighted by the disagreement between the radical John Lilburne and the religious Independent Henry Ireton, regarding how the issue of toleration was to be framed in a document of the army council, the Remonstrance of St. Albans. On the articles concerning toleration, according to Underdown, Ireton, and Lilburne could only meet "half-way." "[Ireton] would deny the magistrate coercive powers to counsel conformity, but would allow restrictive powers to prevent religious practices tending to public disorder."[21] On the other hand, the radicals saw liberty of conscience as a fundamental right that could be supported by natural reason and by Hebraic example in the Old Testament. For the radicals, liberty of conscience assured the freedom to define, worship, and express one's faith without fear of reprisal from ministers or magistrates.[22]

George Bishop reported that he was among those who served to secure the safety of the Commonwealth and liberty of conscience. Fresh from the civil wars and the discussions at Putney, he may have been imbued with a sense of political empowerment when he entered the Commonwealth's service as a sequestration official in Bristol. To his dismay, however, he found that many who had been charged with securing the Commonwealth were misusing their power. A supporter of the Parliamentary purge of December 1648, Bishop had taken a radical stance regarding of the king's execution. He referred to it as a necessity for "the preservation of the public interest."[23] Yet his extant writing reveals an early and steady stream of dissatisfaction with the new Commonwealth. The April 1653 dissolution of the Rump Parliament angered Bishop so deeply that he became an outspoken critic of Cromwell. Thereafter he lost favor, and very likely the trust of the lord general's advisors.

How were the energy and aspirations of radicals like Bishop—soldiers and statesmen who helped fashion political change—redirected after they became alienated from their allies? According to historian Richard Bauman, the intense religiosity and turbulence of mid-seventeenth-century England turned many people to the apocalyptic spirituality of Quakerism as a way of "investing the universe with order."[24] A study of Bishop's work discloses a retreat from politics that was accompanied by a progressive involvement with spiritual matters. His experience serves as a window into the ways in which Quakerism became a repository of disenchanted radicalism.

Chapter 1 explores Bishop's personal background and family connections against a backdrop of the mounting hostilities that lead a reluctant Bristol into the civil war. It also examines his military career and early participation in local politics. In Chapter 2, Bishop's commitment to public affairs, first in Bristol and later at Whitehall, is viewed alongside his awareness that the security of the Commonwealth was being threatened by Parliament's supporters as well as by those of the king. Chapter 3 finds Bishop effectively building the domestic wing of the Commonwealth's intelligence operation. His closeness to the day-to-day affairs of Cromwell, the Council, and the sequestrations committee convince Bishop that the godly Commonwealth was headed for destruction. This chapter ends with a disillusioned Bishop returning to Bristol to live in "a private capacity and retirement." In Chapter 4 Bishop forms ties with the Quakers and becomes involved in the movement's organization. Yet, while remaining loyal to the government and showing an interest in public affairs, he gradually severs his former ties at Whitehall. In Chapter 5 Bishop emerges as a Quaker leader and defender of his faith as he works to reverse the anti-Quaker activity in Bristol, London, and the provinces. In Chapter 6, he continues to petition the authorities for the liberty of conscience that the Quakers need in order to exercise their principles and practices without fear of reprisal. In the spring of 1659 he resumes his interest in London politics when it appears that religious reform might be delivered by the restored Rump. Yet his optimism soon fades as the defeat of "The Good Old Cause" and the fall of the godly Commonwealth become inevitable. The Epilogue traces the development of Bishop's search for liberty of conscience after the 1660 restoration of the King and the passing of the Quaker Act in 1662. It also contrasts Bishop's early Quakerism with the passive resistance he propounded after 1662.

CHAPTER ONE

George Bishop, the New Model
Army Captain from Bristol

MOST OF WHAT WE KNOW about the personal life of George
Bishop, 'Freeman, son of a freeman,' comes to us through his
letters, tracts, and the State Papers. Other details of his life, work,
and thought are found in the words and papers of those with whom
he came in contact as soldier, civil servant, and Quaker. As he 'was
very young when the difference began between the late king and
Parliament,' it is likely that he was born some time during the second
decade of the seventeenth century. Married to Elizabeth Canne in
1648 or 1649, his only surviving child of whom we have record,
Elizabeth, was born in 1655.[25]

   Because his Christian name and his surname were both
common in seventeenth-century England, the question of his exact
identity has commanded the attention of historians. Thankfully, G.
Aylmer, W.A. Cole, J.W. Frost, C. Hill, J.W. Martin, and R.S.
Mortimer have addressed this problem in their work. Their efforts
have established that it was the same George Bishop who served in
the army, worked for the Committee for Examinations, and, upon
his retirement from the civil service, devoted himself to the establishment of Bristol Quakerism.[26] Cole and Hill have identified him
as the Captain Bishop who spoke at Putney.[27] The findings of these
historians dovetail with the autobiographical references in Bishop's
work, which make it unlikely that he was the journalist George Bishop
who ran a London print shop with Robert White in the 1640s.[28]

   His tracts reveal an impressive understanding of Scripture,
history, law, and the classics. This is most evident in his tracts,
A Tender Visitation to Both Universities and *A Looking Glass for the*

Times, which demonstrated a breadth and depth of learning. Nevertheless, he was not a scholar in the conventional sense, and he did not attend Oxford, Cambridge, or the inns of court.[29] As a member of the twenty percent of Bristol's population who were freemen, however, he qualified for admission to one of the city's free grammar schools. According to the ordinances of The Bristol Grammar School, the hours were long, the curriculum rigorous, and the holidays relatively few. Only a handful of artisans' sons went on to university; the rest entered an apprenticeship that lasted for about seven years. Yet it is not surprising that nonacademics like Bishop were fluent in religious dogma. At the grammar school a detailed report of the Sunday sermon was a typical weekly assignment. By Monday the older boys had to write a report on it, and the younger ones were required to present theirs orally. The school required a reading knowledge of English upon entrance; and the syllabus included Nowell's cathechism, as well as Latin and Greek grammar books. Since this was standard fare at the city's grammar schools, we have some insight into the kind of education that was available to Bishop.[30]

He was most likely the son of brewer Thomas Bishop, who was made a burgess on 4 January 1612. Thomas Bishop was successful at his trade, and in 1652 he could afford to pay the considerable sum of five pounds for the rental of town land upon which stood his Corn Street home. George Bishop was made a burgess and 'admitted into the liberties' of the city on 22 September 1649, close in time to his marriage to Elizabeth Canne.[31] There are records of two children born of this marriage: a daughter, Elizabeth, born in 1655; and a newborn son, Benoni, who died in September 1657. Bishop's wife died the following September, and he never remarried. During his ten years of single parenthood, he must surely have depended on the assistance of his unmarried sister, known as Elizabeth Bishop the elder, to care for his daughter. During those years he was deeply involved in Quaker organization and the writing of tracts. He was also jailed three times for refusing to take an oath and give surety of good behavior, and for attending illegal conventicles. He narrowly escaped banishment upon the last conviction.[32] In 1672, four years after George Bishop died, his sister provided young Richard Vickris with 'sufficient certificate ... testifying her assent to consummate the marriage between her niece Elizabeth Bishop and the said Richard.'[33]

9

Both Bishop and his daughter married into families, the Cannes and the Vickrises, who enjoyed mercantile wealth and were among the most politically powerful in Bristol.[34] Their family trees form a tight network of political, mercantile, and religious relationships, bound by blood and perpetuated through marriage. A study of these relations sheds light on the environment in which civil-war politics and early Quakerism flourished. From the experience of Bishop and his son-in-law, Richard Vickris, we learn that having influential relatives did not always protect religious innovators from violence or arrest.

Bishop's wife, Elizabeth, was the daughter of William Canne, who had been regarded as a malignant by the Parliamentarians after they retook the city in 1645. Canne was sheriff in 1636-1637 and mayor in 1648-1649. He became a member of the City Council and an alderman in 1648 and remained in both capacities until his death in March 1658.[35] As a member of the City Council, Canne was a powerful man in Bristol. The Council was the cathedral city's power base, and it wielded more authority than the church. It owned many of the livings in the city, and council members worshiped in high style at their own chapel, which stood near Bristol Cathedral. Yet in spite of the fact that the Council had financial control of lecturers, preachers, and much of church property, they were unable to prevent the appearance of separatist groups before, and especially during, the chaos of the wars.

William Canne was made a burgess upon his August 1620 marriage to Margaret Yeamans, daughter of the merchant and former sheriff Robert Yeamans, who was hanged in 1643 'for conspiring to deliver the city to Prince Rupert.'[36] The Canne family was related through marriage to the Aldworth, Creswick, Hooke, and Yates families. They were aldermen and permanent members of the City Council, and from the 1630s through the 1650s it was frequently their family members who served as mayor and Master of the Merchant Venturers. The men of these families, typical of the merchant-politicians in Sacks's study, monopolized the important posts in the city. Sacks found that nearly sixty percent of the Council elected between 1605 and 1642 were associated with the society of merchants.[37] Canne was master of the Merchant Venturers from 1645 to 1646. This was indeed an important post, because the Merchant Venturers had owned much of the city's wealth and had exercised power since the sixteenth century. Under

10

the protection of a royal charter and the Common Council, it steadily gained control of the local government, as well as the social order of Bristol.[38]

The mercantile and political activities of Elizabeth Canne Bishop's brother, Robert Canne, mirrored that of his father. Both too were implacable enemies of the Quakers. During the mid-1650s, after Quaker preachers John Audland and John Camm gathered followers in Bristol, William and Robert Canne were among those who most staunchly sought to suppress the growth of the movement in the city.

The family that Bishop's daughter married into shared the religious convictions and social status of her Canne relatives. The Vickris family of Bristol and Chew Magna, Somerset, were among the most prosperous merchant families in the West Country. When Elizabeth Bishop and Vickris married in 1672, they were already Quakers. Vickris's grandfather, also Richard Vickris, was born in Bewdley, Worcestershire. A Puritan who sided with the parliamentary army during the civil war, the elder Richard Vickris was elected alderman and mayor in 1646. His son Robert, young Richard's father, served as sheriff in 1656. And like the father and son William and Robert Canne, Richard and Robert Vickris actively pursued the arrest and conviction of Quakers.[39]

Young Richard Vickris, who was probably an only son, was disowned by his family when he became a Quaker. As the heir to a wealthy gentry family, he was surely subject to an enormous amount of pressure when he abandoned the Puritan faith. Vickris authored four tracts and was regarded as a staunch defender of Quakerism. They respected him as a 'sufferer,' one who remains faithful to Quaker principles and practices though exposed to violence or persecution. Under the Recusancy Act of 35 Elizabeth, and upon his refusal to conform, Vickris was sentenced to death. Through the intervention of William Penn, a family friend, the Duke of York was able to secure Vickris a pardon from Judge Jeffries in 1684. Taken with young Richard's character, Penn wrote to the elder Vickris and consoled him for his worldly pains and for the troubles of his son. He assured him that the Lord would be pleased for "the sincere love thou hast shown to thy son and his troubles."[40]

Reconciled with his family, Richard Vickris inherited the family estate of Firgrove in Chew Magna and land in Bristol, Somersetshire, and Gloucestershire. He died in 1700, and

11

Elizabeth Bishop Vickris lived until 1723. Among their large family of some nine or ten children was a son named George and a fourth son named Thomas Bishop. A daughter married into the wealthy gentry Dickinson family and brought with her the Quaker faith, which remained in the family until at least the fourth decade of the eighteenth century.[41]

Himself from more humble origins, Bishop became a brewer in Bristol. He remained in this trade during his Quaker years and perhaps until the end of his life. The city was and still is active in the brewing trade. Today, one can look from Bristol Bridge in the Old City and see evidence of continued local interest in brewing. The view also reveals a natural trade route—along the quay, up the Severn River, and out to sea by way of the Bristol Channel. As the area was the location of the Bristol business district during the seventeenth century, Bishop was at the center of activity in his Corn Street home. The street was the site of the Corn Exchange and the headquarters of the Common Council. It was only a short walk to the Guildhall.

After joining Quakers, perhaps in an effort to justify his efforts to secure liberty of conscience, Bishop reminded the authorities that the civil wars had been fought to redeem the church from the corrupt hold of the king and the bishops.[42] He maintained that the king, bishops, and their supporters had not only denied religious liberty to their Puritan opponents, but had persecuted them so rigorously as to cast them up 'off the face of the earth.'[43] During the late wars, Bishop would argue, it was 'on the bishops' and king's part to oppress [liberty of conscience] and ... on the Parliament's to defend and deliver it.'[44] An exploration of the attitudes and conditions under which Bristol entered the war add dimension to Bishop's comments. What were the prevalent sentiments in his native city toward the king and Parliament? And likewise, to what degree was there a call for religious reform?

According to one account, in 1642 the Common Council unwittingly watched the city get 'dragged reluctantly' into war despite the fact that it never declared for either side. Of the more than two hundred merchants in Bristol, not more than thirty had shown even minimal commitment to one side or the other. And obedience to Parliament's demand that Denzil Holles be admitted to review the trained bands should not be mistaken as a show of enthusiasm.[45]

The fall of the city into royalist hands in 1643, and the numerous fines, petitions, and pardons that followed, suggest that Bristol was sympathetic to the Parliamentary cause. Yet it is curious that, when it built earthworks for defense in November 1643, the only troops in the area belonged to Parliament. Of the thirty merchants who showed any clear partisan interest, twenty had royalist loyalties. Apparently, there were those who thought that, in constitutional and religious matters, the king could not be trusted; others saw Parliament as brazen upstarts. However, despite its reluctance to come to action, on 9 December 1642 Parliamentary forces entered Bristol without the consent of the Common Council.[46]

To gain a better understanding of the prewar attitudes of Bristolians like Bishop, people who had financial interests in the city, we must review the king's actions during the 1620s, a time of economic difficulty and growing unrest in Parliament. Perhaps a mixture of financial need, a dread of Parliaments, and jealousy of Bristol's urban wealth caused Charles in July 1626 to alarm the country about foreign invasion. At the command of the Privy Council, and without cause, Bristol's gates were guarded nightly by trained bands. In an attempt to raise funds, in August 1626 the king ordered Bristol to pay a forced loan. Their resources strained because of England's recent wars with France and Spain, the city merchants failed to comply. Local magistrates felt that the port city had carried a 'disproportionate share of the burden' inasmuch as they not only had lent the king the services of their ships, but also supplied him with money to supply his own.[47] In response to their refusal to grant the loan, the king confirmed the city's charter, an act that required the city merchants to pay obligatory fees.

Such 'galling instrument[s] of extortion,' we are told, continued through the 1630s. In 1637 an unpopular audit of the city merchants' collection records was conducted by royal commissioners. Allegedly, evidence was fabricated by them that 'turned friend against friend,' and under the guise of reform several trades were subjected to additional fees. The commissioners also estimated the amount of business that merchants could expect and then audited their records weekly. In Bishop's trade, "The brewer was enjoined to pay forty marks a year for a commission, of all which the poor commons do feel the smart."[48]

During the last three months of 1637, royal commissioners subjected other trades, including soapmakers, ministers, constables, and shipowners, to similar scrutiny. One source reported that

> Our city was never [then] free from commissions, commissioners and pursuivants of sundry sorts, which lay in several parts of our city to make inquiry not only against merchants but against tradesmen, who were examined and sent up to London, and great impositions laid on them to the grief of many.[49]

Once the war had begun, four aldermen presented the king with various grievances, including the innovations that the prelates had imposed upon the Church of England. The Puritans in the city complained of the ignorance and lack of discipline that characterized the church and its ministers. It seems that there was more than a modicum of unrest in the trading city over political, economic, and religious maneuverings that threatened the privileges it regarded as rights. The climate in which Bishop joined the Parliamentary army supports the assertion of one modern historian, who found that the civil wars were caused by a complex combination of religious and constitutional issues.[50] Yet it must be maintained that Bristol sought to remain aloof from the impending struggle. In a show of defiance, the city refused to let in royal troops, explaining that the king had not given the command. Likewise, the request to keep Frome Gate closed was ignored when—as the story goes—'by a woman's trick' it was opened, letting Essex and his troops enter the city.[51] Once hostilities began, the royalist mayor and sheriffs worked to sabotage the transport of troops and arms into Somerset.[52]

Bristol's fate during the war has often been repeated. Initially held by the Parliamentary army, the city was surrendered by Nathaniel Fiennes to Prince Rupert in 1643, an act for which he came under great criticism and for which he narrowly escaped death. Riding upon the crest of success and fresh from the taking of Sherburn Castle, Bristol fell to Fairfax's forces after a two-day battle in September 1645. The casualties were large and the destruction ruinous. Underdown has noted that Rupert's two thousand troops "were not of the best quality and the citizens [of Bristol] were demoralized and apathetic."[53] The articles of surrender reveal a stiff cordiality that masked fears of reprisal. Both sides bargained hard to maintain safety and dignity. But there was no doubt about who had been defeated and in whose direction fortune had nodded her head.[54]

For merchants like Bishop, the struggle caused devastating financial inconvenience, along with the usual miseries that accompanied early modern warfare—general disruption, pillaging, and a bout of plague. In postwar Bristol, according to Bishop, the plague caused 'upwards of one hundred [deaths] a week.'[55] It is understandable that his neighbors wanted a return to the normality that would revive trade and a peaceful existence. Cromwell recalled how for the army at Sherburn there was: 'Some inducement to bring us thither [to Bristol] ... at the report of the good affection of the townsmen to us.'[56] During the war a group of Parliament supporters from Bristol addressed the king concerning the practices of his ministers and bishops that had resulted in such ruinous conditions. Hoping for a quick peace, they complained that Bristol's ships 'lie rotting in the harbor without any mariners ... or trade into foreign parts by reason of our home-bred distractions.'[57] The protests that Bishop wrote after the wars would echo their complaints that the destructive power of the bishops had forced new and unheard of doctrines upon the people. They specified,

> No oppression [was] so forcible or oppressive to men's consciences as that which is intruded on them concerning their belief.[58]

This accusation was not left unanswered. Shortly thereafter, the king's secretary, Lord Falkland, delivered the royal reply:

> The abuses and innovations [that] have lately happened in the Church of England to the grievance of many men's conscience, his majesty declares that he is ignorant of ... so he will be always ready to expunge and take away all such innovations: being resolute as he is Defender of the Faith, to ... maintain no other religion but the orthodox established doctrine of the Church of England which

hath so flourished under the reigns of his
glorious predecessors that for the inso-
lence and pride of the prelacy.[59]
     And thus the war continued, with each side seeing itself as
the defender of the faith and liberties of England.
     The experience of war, particularly his marching out of
Bristol with Parliament's forces when the city fell to the royalists
in 1643 and not returning until 'the city was retaken by Parliament,'
must have had a powerful impact on Bishop's life.[60] His concern
for his native city would become a recurrent theme in his work.
Before he returned to the city, Bishop fought at the Battle of Naseby,
where three thousand Parliamentary troops faced some seven thousand royalist counterparts. In June 1645 Bishop reported
Parliament's victory over Prince Rupert's troops to Lieutenant
Colonel Roe. Like other reports of the battle, which marked the
turning point in the war, Bishop's account seems to have been
aimed at rallying the spirits of the war-weary soldiers. Bishop
underscored how the regiments' valor and keen sense of logistics
occasioned the royalist retreat.[61]
     Written at Great Glen, which lies to the northwest of
Naseby in the direction of Leicestershire, Bishop may have
composed his report while en route to the site of the army's next
victory. In an elated mood, he provided Roe with the regimental
breakdown of this victorious battle, which had come about despite
the advantages held by the royalists. Both the king and Cromwell
had been injured at Naseby. The king had suffered a wound to his
right arm. and Cromwell had lost his headpiece, leaving him 'within
push of pike.' The deepest drama in the narrative was the account
of how Maj. Philip Skippon, Bishop's "dear friend," had suffered
a serious wound to his ribs yet fought on for two and one-half hours,
until the field had been won.[62]
     To Bishop, God's will had brought about the victory at
Naseby. God had placed the sword of righteousness in the appro-
priate godly hands. Among the attendant Parliamentary chaplains
was Hugh Peter, who 'with bible and pistol in either hand, rode
from rank to rank with strident exhortation in his role as warrior
priest.'[63] Bishop's metaphorical use of death serves as a striking
contrast to the tract's congratulatory tone.

I believe the good success God hath given
us, how he raised us out of our graves and

caused our dead hopes to live again ... not
withstanding our wounds and our weary
men in this great battle, which may be the
saving of the[se] three kingdoms.[64]

According to Bishop, General Fairfax, the commanding
officer, had 'looked like a dead man' before the battle began. Their
adversaries had formerly 'scoff[ed]' at the New Model's disunity.
Nonetheless, Bishop felt assured that 'the hand of God' would soon
bring them victory.[65] The victory at Naseby apparently left a
profound impression on the soldiers. Woolrych comments that

out of the ferment of preaching and the
heat of battle would soon be forged a
genuine revolutionary spirit radical in
politics and in religion, and poles apart
from the limited, lawyer-like objections
which the Long Parliament had first set
itself. Naseby ... gave this army ... its
baptism of fire.[66]

Yet despite their success, the army was becoming increasingly discontented. A second war seemed inevitable, because negotiations with the king were proving fruitless. Uncertainty about the
future aggravated their present conditions: The soldiers were
unpaid and therefore unable to afford the high price of food that
was occasioned by a poor harvest.[67] In March 1647 Parliament
sent agents to army headquarters at Saffron Walden to recruit men
for Ireland. The army seemed on the brink of revolt. At the end of
May, both the officers and rank and file rejected the Parliamentary
order to disband.

During the first week of June, they bound themselves
together in a pact, the Solemn Engagement of the Army. The
Engagement was written to inform Parliament that the army would
neither disperse nor fight in Ireland until their demands were met.
Their primary concern was for payment of arrears, freedom from
future impressment, and compensation for the wounded and their
families.[68] The encamped forces at Newmarket, united and with
the reluctant solidarity of Fairfax, created the General Council of
the Army. Two officers and two soldiers from each regiment were
to be included in the Council. It was charged with defining and
adjudicating the differences between the army and parliament. The

Engagement also provided for the election of 'general agitators.' They would review proposals from the various regiments and present them to the army's high command.[69]

There were also numerous disagreements between the soldiers and their commanding officers. The soldiers' unrest was created in part by the Levellers, a group of radicals, including John Lilburne, Richard Overton, and John Wildman, who proposed a version of democratic reform. Along with various proposals for social reform, the Levellers sought to broaden the franchise and secure freedom of conscience. Their ideas were embodied in their constitution-like document, the Agreement of the People. The reforms in the Agreement were considered excessive by the more moderate officers. By whipping up discontent among the soldiers, the Levellers hoped to form a united front in opposition to their superiors. Their October 1647 tract, *The Case of the Army Truly Stated* reminded the rank and file that they might soon be disbanded without receiving their arrears or a guarantee against future service. Moreover, they were warned that they would suffer severely if the king were set free, since they had never received indemnity for their wartime activity. To mitigate the mounting unrest of their troops, the high command formed a council to meet with the agitators who had been appointed by the Solemn Engagement.[70]

In October and November 1647, in a climate of growing discontent, the army held a series of debates on the outskirts of London, at Putney Church. The Putney debates are mostly remembered for the discussions about democratic principles. However, the question of how the conflict in the kingdom would be settled was perhaps the most pressing concern of Bishop and others who aired their views.

Bishop may have traveled to Putney from Bristol with some of the army's high command. He had moved among them since at least 1645, when he dressed Skippon's wound and gathered the details for his historical tract of the battle. Upon his return to Bristol in 1645, he continued his association with the army officers and may have gained their recognition through his involvement in local affairs. Seeing Bristol 'miserably torn with wars and factions,' Bishop was successful in his efforts to have Colonel Charles Fleetwood appointed governor.[71] Bishop thought Fleetwood was capable of restoring 'calm and friendly favor about the sterility that was over ... Bristol through the harshness of the rough storms that

18

had compassed it about.'[72] Bishop had also made the acquaintance of General Fairfax when, through his 'natural love to the city of Bristol,' he petitioned him to reduce the number of troops who were depriving the city of scarce resources.[73] Long past Putney, indeed until the eve of the restoration of the king, Bishop continued his association with the army officers. This was most evident in 1654, when they protected the Quakers who began to appear in Bristol, and again in 1659 when the army's intervention in Parliamentary affairs looked hopeful for the Quakers.

Interpreting recent events as the manifestation of God's will and obedience to providence as people's main obligation[74], Bishop's first speech at Putney addressed the problem of preserving the war-torn kingdom. Using contemporary religion, he indicted their indifference to God's will as an invitation to disaster. He told the troubled soldiers that their disunity was sabotaging their attempt to settle the kingdom. God, he cautioned, would regard their disunity as poor recompense for having placed the sword of victory in their hands. His comments at Putney foreshadowed his Quaker concern for the destruction that results from the preoccupation with self-interest and the temptations of this world. His assessment that 'God is not pleased to come unto you'[75] is striking as it anticipated the central Quaker concept of the inner light. His comments at Putney were driven by an already present conviction that eternal truth is made available to human intellect through the divine intervention of Christ.

Bishop believed God had been angered by the army's failure to seal its victory with a peaceful settlement. Self-interest had prevented it from doing so. In support of his statement, he referred his listeners to the letter that the mystic preacher John Saltmarsh had written to the army council. It read:

> You have not discharged yourselves to the people in such things as they justly expected from you and for which you had that spirit of righteousness first put upon you by an Almighty Power ... The wisdom of the flesh had deceived and enticed ... And now you are met in council (I hope) the Lord make you to hearken to one another from the highest to the meanest,

that the voice of God, wheresoever it
speaks, may not be despised ... Look over
your first engagements and compare them
with your proceedings, that you may see
what you have done.[76]

Bishop also participated in the discussion of how the king
should be brought to justice. After the conclusion of the first wars
in June 1646, negotiations with the king proved fruitless. The king
had been handed to the army by the Scottish soldiers to whom he
had given himself up in May 1646. Parliament and the army had
offered Charles their respective proposals for concluding peace. Yet
there was no real movement to bring the king to trial for treason
until late 1648, at which time it became evident that he had been
deceitful in his negotiations with Parliament and the army. During
the Putney debates he was in the army's custody on the Isle of
Wight, from where he would soon escape to seek an army that
would restore him to power.[77]

At Putney Bishop was among those radicals who were
against further negotiations with the king and who were beginning
to advocate strong measures for dealing with him. In November he
and a group of agitators contacted the House and expressed their
disapproval, which they afterwards modified concerning
'Parliament's sending propositions to the king.'[78]

In his second recorded comment at Putney, Bishop
returned to the question of the preservation of the kingdom. He
also returned to the idea of divinely inspired internal truth. The
army had been unable to save the kingdom, he explained, from its
'dying condition' because, as long as Charles Stuart was king, God
would remain angry. He said this had been made known to him
'after many inquiries in[to] . . . [his] spirit.'[79] He concluded that
it was a destructive compliance 'to preserve that man of blood and
those principles of tyranny which God from heaven by many
successes hath manifestly declared against.'[80] Bishop was careful
to include that his sentiments stemmed primarily from his spirituality, not from his politics. He remarked, 'I say not [this] in respect
of any particular persons. I only speak this [as] what is upon my
spirit.'[81]

Hill comments on how, in later years, after his conversion
to Quakerism, Bishop maintained the position that the king had
been the author of his own destruction.[82] Bishop would assert that

20

there had been no recourse in 1649 but to have 'justice done on the king and ... change the government thereupon.'[83] Indeed, Bishop cautioned the newly restored Charles II to 'do the thing which is holy ... which is righteous unto all, for the sake of the righteousness of God (which we know hath been revealed in judgment on the unrighteous before thee).'[84]

Some time after the Putney debates, Bishop returned to Bristol still in active military service, yet sufficiently involved with brewing to supply the army with beer for its expedition to Ireland.[85] He also maintained the interest in public affairs that he had exhibited at Putney. For the next seven years he was employed in the state's service, locally at first, then moving on to Whitehall in 1650. Aylmer included Bishop among the remarkable individuals who had not been to university or to one of the inns of court yet were talented enough to secure 'excellent openings' in the civil service during the 1640s.[86]

CHAPTER TWO

Entering the Commonwealth's Civil Service: From Bristol to Whitehall

AFTER THE JANUARY 1649 execution of King Charles I, the English government was in disarray. During the previous December, a majority in Parliament had expressed satisfaction over the negotiations with the king, to the chagrin of the MPs and soldiers who believed that he must be removed from power. The purging of the obstructionist MPs in December 1648 by Colonel Thomas Pride and his troopers rendered a 'Rump' of fifty-six members who subsequently transformed England into a Commonwealth. Those who sought to compromise with the king were either prohibited from taking their seats or imprisoned if they protested loudly.[87]

The new House of Commons was scarcely one-fourth the size of the previous body. We have learned that it was composed of MPs with varying shades of Presbyterian or Independent sentiments. Yet the radicals must have looked upon it as the instrument that would install the much-needed political and religious reforms. Those, like Bishop, who hoped that the removal of the king would 'deliver ... the liberties of the nation' soon learned that, before the Commonwealth could be free to devote itself to political and religious reform, it must concentrate on protecting itself from the foreign and domestic-based royalist and Presbyterian plots that had been designed to enthrone young Charles Stuart as Charles II.[88] Thus, to guarantee its own survival, the new commonwealth made the collection of intelligence, not the initiation of reform, its primary task.

One of the first acts of the Rump Parliament, the body which sat between Pride's purge and Cromwell's 20 April 1653 dissolution, was to establish a new executive office—the Council of State. As the highest of the various Parliamentary committees that conducted the Commonwealth's affairs, it was composed of members of the army's high command and those whom the army had allowed to remain in the House of Commons. During the next few years, Bishop gathered intelligence for a committee under the direction of the Council, the Committee for Examinations and Discoveries. The Committee provided the Council with information and testimony. If the evidence they reviewed was substantial, the suspect was tried by the Parliamentary court. If he was found guilty, his estate was "compounded" or "sequestered," that is, fined or confiscated.

Bishop remained active in the army until the September 1650 Battle of Dunbar; yet, since his 1645 return to Bristol, he had been reporting local intelligence to army officers, including Maj.-Gen. Thomas Harrison and Capt. Edward Sexby. Well informed in local affairs, he became a local commissioner in the West Country. Bishop's civic involvement was surely sparked by the combination of his concern for 'the liberties of the nation' and the contemporary idea of 'neighborliness.' Wrightson has found that, in the provinces, 'effective equals,' that is, trusted members of 'the moral community,' were bound by custom to resolve conflict and safeguard community interests.[89] Bristol, it must be remembered, was a city that had a sizable population who were royalist supporters.[90] Naturally, upon the establishment of the new Commonwealth, they experienced a sense of loss and insecurity when ancient traditions and institutions were ignored or replaced. Bishop's involvement in local affairs can best be understood as an example of the amateur, often unpaid, local officials whose 'diligence and cooperation' became essential to the maintenance of order.[91]

As a local intelligence official, Bishop learned that men who had formerly fought with the godly army were suspected of corruption and of disobeying Parliamentary orders concerning the resources in the Forest of Dean. In response he wrote that pretended Parliamentary servants and former commissioners had 'boasted that they have cut down four hundred trees contrary to an order of Parliament, and notoriously abuse and scandalize those that through abundance of toil have brought those spoils to light.'[92]

23

The Forest of Dean, a former royal preserve that covers some 30,000 acres in West Gloucestershire, lies in a fertile area between the Severn and Wye Rivers. Before the first wars the forest was in the hands of Sir John Winter, who had received the rights to its use through a royal grant. Winter himself ravaged its rich natural resources and disregarded the 16,000 pound annual usage fee.[93]

The 'turbulent' inhabitants of the forest, 'constant friends of the Parliament,' had resisted Winter's royalist troops during the wars.[94] In 1648 Cromwell and Parliament took steps to preserve the forest and to stop the lawlessness and pillaging that accompanied the civil war. On 19 April 1648, Parliament passed an ordinance for the preservation of timber in the Forest of Dean. Yet a group including several army officers and preservators disregarded the order and added to the destruction of the some 50,000 trees that had been lost since Winter was stripped of his rights to it in 1641.[95]

In December 1649, experiencing what was perhaps his first political disenchantment with the Commonwealth, Bishop and Col. Brownwick reported this situation to Parliament. This report was among the many accounts of corruption that Whitehall received in response to the local officials they employed in the counties who were connected to central committees in London. Parliament and the Council of State recognized that the unwillingness 'of others of a better quality' to serve sometimes occasioned the appointment of 'persons of inferior rank.'[96] Complaints from the counties called for the discontinuance of these committees, as 'they have abused and, in an arbitrary manner, oppressed the people to the scandal of the Parliament.'[97] This situation exposed Bishop, a Parliamentary soldier and official himself, to the disappointment that is often experienced by revolutionaries when it becomes clear that corruption and discord exist among their allies.

Bishop was indignant that the preservators had disregarded the need to preserve the forest's resources, which were essential to Bristol's trading interests. He reported that, in addition to the illegal felling of trees, the preservators had disregarded the usual standard of quality and pricing of wood. Bishop was most outraged that, although the forest officials were 'friends of the Parliament,' Col. Kerle and Capts. Pury, Grifford, Brome, and Philips had 'scorned and disobeyed' orders and bribed cutters, who performed

24

the actual destruction. Incensed at Bishop's report, the violators attempted to discredit Bishop and his associates.[98]

In an effort to clear his name and to inform the public of the officers' wrong doing, Bishop wrote *A Modest Check to Part of a Most Scandalous Libel*. In this tract, Bishop vented his self-righteous outrage for which 'the authors' of such mischiefs [deserved] exemplary punishment.'[99] His comments suggest that many of these officials were feigning religiosity to serve their own political and personal interests.

Bishop's ideas are highlighted by Raab's finding that at no time before 1640 or after 1660 was English political thought so influenced by 'Machiavellian ideas and criteria of political action and judgment.'[100] A key component of this thought, Raab found, was the utilization of God as 'a political device.'[101] In light of the violators' behavior, Bishop wrote that they were deceiving both God and country. 'I could wish they had as much conscience to God and men as they have to their own interest, for which it may be feared they make religion a cloake, which God in time will discover.'[102] To his outrage, they had also 'disobeyed the orders of the state [that had been made to prevent those destructions... called them hedge orders and the commission under the new great seal a hedge commission.'[103]

There was another local situation that caused Bishop to once again challenge those with whom he had sided in the wars. As another demonstration of service to the 'moral community,' Bishop joined the Bristol branch of the Committee for Sequestrations some time after 1645. Formed by Parliamentary ordinance in 1643, the local committees were created to compound the estates of prelates and papists.[104] Before long, the committees were empowered to act against those who supported the king in his struggle with Parliament. The sequestration committees employed soldiers who were now regarded as a menace by the war-weary people and were the focus of numerous complaints.[105] Perhaps the most hated of the county committees under Parliament's supervision, the sequestration committee proved effective at sapping the strength of royalist conspirators.[106] Reportedly, the committee collected in excess of 1,304,957 pounds. The funds helped pay for 'the supportation of the great charges of the Commonwealth, and for the easing of the good subjects, who have hitherto borne the greatest share in these burdens.'[107]

As was true with other victories, the 1645 Parliamentary retaking of Bristol exposed the army and Parliament to the threat of counterattack by those who were loyal to the king. In Bristol, where royalist support was great and where there was an acute fear of loyalists, Parliament shook its fist in the form of stiff liens on royalist property. Thus the state's policy of composition and sequestration also served as a preventative measure.

The royalist sequestration affair in Bristol, in which Bishop represented the accused loyalists' interests to the local committee and to Parliament, lasted from 1646 to 1650. Interestingly, accusations coincided with a change in power on the City Council and competition for local office and representation in London. When Bishop returned to Bristol in 1645, the city was being ravaged by the plague and torn apart by political factions. Shortly after Bishop secured Col. Charles Fleetwood's appointment as governor, some Bristolians, possibly offended by Fleetwood's reputation for befriending sectaries, petitioned Whitehall for a replacement. The insecurity of local political appointments in Bristol is reflective of the larger situation that existed during the civil wars and the Interregnum. Morrill, Underdown, and Wrightson have presented numerous instances of discontent with the new political order that expressed itself in a readiness to challenge or ignore new appointments and political innovations.[108]

An influential group of citizens was attracted to Skippon's reputation for keeping the peace in potentially volatile situations. They ousted Fleetwood from office. Yet according to Bishop, Fleetwood had been successful at quieting the city, claiming it was sheer factionalism that had caused his dismissal. He remained a supporter of Fleetwood through the wars and during the Commonwealth and Protectorate.

Bishop also noted that, in general, political replacements were being made according to the 'private commodity and advantage of some particular persons who as horse leeches suck the breasts of the opportunity to serve their purpose, dividing the city into factions for that end under the pretense of the public.'[109] Three aldermen who had been royalist sympathizers—Creswick, Hooke, and James—were displaced from office and placed under threat of composition. This had been done despite the fact that they had already contributed to the 6,000-pound ransom to the army that was supposed to secure their safety.

Bishop explained his motivation for lending assistance to his fellow Bristolians in a way that connects and lends imagery to Wrightson's findings that 'neighborliness' was a

> virtue which stood 'perhaps first in the criteria by which the social and ethical standing of an individual was measured' ... Aid and support [was] rendered to one another by neighbors, services which might often enough be vitally important to people who shared an environment which could be chronically insecure.[110]

In this case, according to Bishop, factionalism was the source of the insecure situation. In a January 1651 letter to Cromwell written ostensibly on Hooke's behalf, Bishop declared that he had 'nothing in this but conscience.' He was concerned about the hardships that had fallen upon the city merchants who, he argued, had been 'with the contrary party during the war.' The sequestrations jeopardized the royalist supporters' reputations and livelihoods, while the wolfish Londoners watched and waited to move in on their prosperity.[111]

While Bishop petitioned the cases of his fellow Bristolians to the Committee for Compositions, he was already in the employ of the Council of State.[112] With the assistance of his cousin, lawyer John Haggett, he successfully worked past the bureaucratic stumbling blocks that were prolonging the threat of sequestration to the accused malignants. At his own expense, and with the limited assistance of others, the young brewer brought the matter to the attention of the officers of the army, associates with whom he obviously had influence.

He continued to secure letters of support from Fairfax and Cromwell. He then petitioned the thirteen-member Parliamentary Committee for the West and reasoned that the sequestrations violated the fourth article of Bristol's terms of surrender. At the local level, he was able to 'cut through a mass of detail and state the relevant findings effectively.'[113] Throughout the ordeal, Parliament kept a watchful eye on Bristol, and intelligence reports disclosed that there was no mischief brewing. Parliament and the Council of State also received reports of Bristol's loyalty from Naval Commissioner Sir Henry Vane, the city's High Steward. The religious Independent Vane had assisted Bishop in this matter, and we can hence date from this time the association that in 1659 would join them in an effort to secure liberty of conscience.

Yet the affair dragged on until the victory at Worcester, when it was resolved as part of the Act of Indemnity. Under this act, former royalist sympathizers were released from jeopardy of composition or sequestration. This was particularly helpful to the Bristolians whose fines for their pre-1645 actions were still pending. The delays that resulted from Bishop's efforts enabled his fellow citizens to benefit from the 1651 act. He claimed that he had so thoroughly convinced leading MPs, including Lord Commissioner Whitelocke, Sir Henry Vane, Sir Arthur Haselrig, Col. Henry Marten, the Lord Commissioner Lisle, and Lord Chief Justice St. Johns,

> that if the instructions for the Act of Indemnity, and the general pardon in general did not reach Bristol in particular, Bristol should have a particular act of indemnity for itself ... [they] ordered the petition and considerations annexed to be left in the hands of the clerk of the House for that purpose.[114]

Bishop sat in the lobby while the House voted on the Act of Indemnity. As a gesture of thanks for assisting fellow members in this affair, and for his assistance with an unrelated matter that cleared them of a 20,000-pound legal suit, the Bristol branch of the Society of Merchant Venturers made Bishop an honorary member. They recorded that, after 'taking into consideration the many factors and courtesies done unto this Company by Mr. George Bishop at London ... [we] admit the said Mr. Bishop a free burgess of this society.'[115]

Before the matter of royalist compositions in Bristol was concluded, and perhaps because as a local commissioner he had become a familiar face in London, Bishop was made Secretary to the Committee for Examinations at Whitehall. In September 1650, he was called to London 'to pursue some business already begun by him ... diverting him from his own occasion to pursue [that] of the public.'[116] When he joined the London circle of politicians who were shaping reform, Bishop gained the opportunity to deepen his commitment to public affairs. Through his daily contact with members of Parliament, the Council, and high-ranking officials, he would have a voice in the political life of the nation. Moreover, his position gave him a deeper understanding of the policies of those who were closest to power and intensified whatever concerns for political and religious reform he had brought with him from Bristol. Before long he would ask fundamental questions about peace and security.

When he left Bristol, however, Bishop may have left behind some enemies he made in the postwar affairs. He felt that his work on behalf of the displaced officials and the royalist supporters added to the suspicions that surrounded him when he joined the Quakers. Many who had fought for Parliament during the wars, and whom Bishop had accused of creating factions and acting against the best interests of the city, were in power when he returned to the city during or soon after November 1654. Remembering the stir he created before he left Whitehall, they looked at him with 'squint of eye.'[117]

Under the directorship of the Council of State, the Committee for Examinations was the intelligence-gathering wing of the Committee for Compounding with Delinquents that had existed since 1644, and which in April 1650 had been reorganized as the Committee for Sequestrations and Advancement of Money for Compounding Delinquents.[118] It was the Committee's function to bring forth delinquents to compounders, to secure a confession and a pledge of loyalty to the 'present government.'[119] As such, it served the dual purpose of discouraging rebellion and raising much-needed revenue. As Secretary to the Committee for Examinations, Bishop would be paid the sizable sum of 200 pounds a year, plus expenses, for his services by the Council's secretary, Walter Frost.[120]

On 13 January 1651, less than one year after his appointment, Bishop was empowered by the Council of State

> to hold intelligence with persons fit for discovering conspiracies against the Commonwealth, which intelligence he is to communicate to the Committee for Examinations, to be used for the public advantage, and sums conceived necessary by the said committee, for enabling Capt. Bishop to gain intelligence are to be paid

by Mr. Frost to him upon their orders, for which he is to give account.[121]

Initially hired to cross-examine suspects, Bishop's position soon involved him 'in ferreting out possible royalist conspirators.'[122] Thus, during the next few years, Bishop's life revolved around the safeguarding of the Commonwealth from those who sought to destroy it. The extant documents invariably portray Bishop as a loyal, vigilant civil servant who called for tough treatment of delinquents and conspirators. Yet he was not without mercy, since he made the distinction 'between repenting men and those that go astray and will not harken to return.'[123] His hard-line policy consistently surfaces from his correspondence and the recorded reactions of his contemporaries. This is especially true in the three cases that most clearly illustrate Bishop's role as a civil servant of the Commonwealth: the Norfolk insurrection; the confiscation case of William, Lord Craven; and the trial and execution of the Presbyterian minister Christopher Love.

In each case Bishop worked alongside his immediate supervisor, Thomas Scot. In July 1649, Scot was appointed by the Council of State at a fee of 800 pounds per year to manage the intelligence for the state both at home and abroad. According to Scot, Bishop was hired to assist him in his role of guarding the Commonwealth against royalist plots. Bishop managed the domestic end of intelligence, while Scot oversaw foreign operations. Their partnership ended shortly after Cromwell's April 1653 dissolution of the Rump Parliament. Both Scot and Bishop worked closely with agents in their employ and with members of the army and government, like Harrison and Maj.-Gen. John Lambert, whose services were conscripted by the Council of State in their all-out effort to secure the Commonwealth's safety. Scot resumed intelligence activities after the army restored the Rump in 1659, along with former colleagues, including Bishop's associates Vane and Fleetwood.[124]

Bishop presented cases of accused conspirators to the High Court of Justice that had been created in January 1649 to try the king. Judge John Bradshaw presided over the Court, and Bishop admired his integrity and capability. Apparently, the Committee and the Court worked closely, and Bishop found himself well enough informed of Bradshaw's service to the Commonwealth to lecture Cromwell on his associate's behalf. After Bradshaw's death,

Bishop was reportedly in possession of his papers. In March 1662 Charles II would write the mayor of Bristol, that one George Bishop had 'divers papers and writings taken by Bradshaw "out of the king's library at Whitehall, which could not yet be recovered."'[125]

Bishop brought to his work a devotion and energy that would later characterize his Quakerism. In his post at Whitehall, and in later years as a Quaker, he demonstrated a tense concern for the safety of the godly Commonwealth. When he entered public office, he may have had a program of religious reform in mind; however, the Commonwealth's safety appears to have been his primary concern. Along with other radicals, Bishop knew that, if the king returned, all hope of reform—religious or otherwise—would be lost.

Throughout the Interregnum, royalist conspiracy was a serious problem. Eventually it played a hand in the events that resulted in the return of the king.[126] Disruption, displacement, and the unwelcome centralization of local affairs that was often accompanied by corruption made much of the country apathetic or hostile to the new regime.[127] And thus, with so much at stake, the radical civil servants Scot and Bishop hired numerous informants who were said to be 'swarming over all England as lice and frogs did Egypt.'[128] The royalists themselves, often to an undercover agent, would comment on the irksomeness of the Commonwealth's spies. One royalist complained: 'He (Scot) do think you deal with the devil, that as soon as a thing be thought of, you know them.' Yet little did the Marquis of Newcastle know that he was talking to one of Bishop's own agents.[129] By the astute use of secret agents, intensive interrogations of captured royalist plotters, and other traditional techniques, such as the expert deciphering by Dr. John Wallis of Oxford, they broke up one conspiracy after another before it could result in effective rebellion.

Bishop soon discovered that he had walked into a tense situation that was created by the May 1650 agreement between Charles II and the Commission of General Assembly of the Kirk of Scotland. Under the terms of what is known as the Treaty of Breda, the Scottish Commissioners pledged their help to Charles II in his struggle to regain the throne. He, in turn, reluctantly agreed to several Presbyterian concessions.

Bishop also learned that the country was still threatened by those who planned the July 1650 royalist insurrection in Norfolk, an unsuccessful attempt at toppling the Commonwealth and returning Charles II. Rumors were about that the area would again be the stage of royalist insurrection. The July riots had been swiftly squashed by the Parliamentary forces under Colonel Rich. The leaders were executed on order of the High Court of Justice, since the magistrates recognized that no local court would execute them.[130]

Moved by talk of some 1,500 men who were waiting to rise and, with the king and a Scottish army, retake England, Bishop wrote to Thomas Scot that the July outbreak had been but a prelude to a major insurrection. The conspirators plotted to slip Charles back into England; with the assistance of Newcastle and others, including four thousand German mercenaries, the royalist forces would secure themselves in the north. Bishop's messengers reported that a major uprising was scheduled to take place before Christmas 1650 under the direction of Newcastle and Lieut. Gen. Carpe. They would land in Kent and quickly place a network of officers throughout England. A double agent whom Bishop kept close to Newcastle, one Mrs. Hamlin, was to bring Cromwell a ciphered letter meant for the king.[131]

Like the Treaty of Breda, the Norfolk Insurrection was largely planned from the exiled king's court in Holland. Two central figures in both affairs were the wealthy royalists William, Lord Craven and William Cavendish, the Marquis of Newcastle. Both men were regularly seen in the king's company by agents charged with observing their movements. Lord Craven, in exile since 1641, was an intimate friend of the king's aunt, Elizabeth Stuart, dowager Queen of Bohemia.[132] According to the report of Bishop's agent, Maj. Richard Falconer, Craven played a part in the drafting of the Treaty of Breda and, like Newcastle, was involved in the Norfolk insurrection.[133]

In the weeks before the conclusion of the Treaty of Breda, Falconer had frequently observed Craven and Newcastle in the presence of the king. Having little stomach for the Scots and their insistence that the king guarantee a reformation of the English church along strict Presbyterian lines, the royalists had initially hoped to restore the king by combining their resources with foreign support and loyalty at home. Bishop knew that the alliance between the Presbyterians and royalists was merely one of convenience. He commented: 'Under the route at Dunbar, the royal party were much comforted in seeing us destroy their enemy, as well as ours.'[134]

Although in Norfolk and other areas the royalists continued to reverse the political situation on their own, they now began
to take a forced interest in the negotiations between Charles and
the Scots. Gardiner comments that 'the negotiations between
Charles and the Scots caused no slight alarm at Westminster; all
the more it seemed probable that the English Presbyterians who
had stood aloof from the royalists in 1648 might now throw in their
lot with them in 1650.'[135]   As a double agent, Falconer was asked
by some thirty royalist officers to deliver a petition to the king pledg-
ing their services to him in his Scottish negotiations. Penned by
Craven, the petition referred to those who had deposed Charles I
as 'the barbarous and inhuman rebels.'

With the fragile Commonwealth surrounded by royalist plots,
a phrase like this was bound to inflame those in power. Craven was
branded an enemy of the Commonwealth, and his estates came under
the review of the Committee for Compounding with Delinquents.
Yet during the latter part of 1650, Bishop's main concern for the
Commonwealth was not Craven; it centered on Newcastle's
involvement in the anticipated second insurrection in Norfolk.

Bishop made numerous reports on the Norfolk situation to
the Council of State, while his agents sought to sabotage the
conspirators' plans. Consequently, the Council asked Parliament
to prohibit sports events that might be staged to mask military gatherings. They also recommended that troops be sent to the north in
preparation for an insurrection from Scotland.[136] Whether invasion was averted as a result of these preventative measures, or
whether it never materialized because Bishop 'overestimated the
enemy's preparedness,' remains a mystery.[137]

Yet Bishop's alarm was not without a basis. In January 1651,
his agents gathered several letters from two royalist agents, Freeman
and Staff. Through coded language, they revealed a network of
supporters who were actively coordinating invasion. Undaunted by
the misfiring of their efforts for a December 1650 insurrection, they
were confident that, if they acquired the necessary funding and
support of Sweden and Brandenburg, things 'will be extremely
advantageous to the king, if [the king's supporters] do not miss the
time of acting. I am sure they have considered strength, and will
carry all.'[138] The royalists anticipated a wide-scale invasion from
abroad, backed by the readiness of several English districts. Bishop
reported to Scot on December 24: 'It seems Dover is designated

and upon that surprise, four thousand Dutch and English are to land in Kent under the command ... of Newcastle (for we have a letter in his hand to the king wherein he begs it) and Lt. Gen. Carpe, then the country will rise.'[139]

Bishop sent Cromwell intercepted letters and added: 'A party of horse were to step out of Scotland into England, then all on that side of the Trent were to rise at once: The eastern Association immediately in one night, Kent, Surrey and Sussex three nights after that, and the west seven nights later.'[140] They had learned that the country was divided into districts, each having an appointed commander and supporters who would rise when the time was right. Evidence gathered at an arrest in March would confirm this situation and clarify that the exiled leaders, primarily Newcastle and Craven, had been among the chief organizers and supporters of the local associations. Newcastle himself was in charge of the Northern Association. Craven lent financial support to the king's cause in the early 1650s, continuing to do so until the Restoration, by which time his contributions totaled some 50,000 pounds.

In February 1651, Falconer dictated a report to Bishop that outlined Craven's treasonous act of petitioning the king to negotiate with the Scots. Falconer's account, including Craven's reference to the Commonwealth as 'barbarous and inhuman rebels' was corroborated by agents Riley and Kitchener. In March 1651, the three examinations were presented to Parliament. The agents came under great criticism from Craven's supporters in Holland. Inevitably, their credibility as witnesses was attacked, and their lives were in danger. Riley's career as a mercenary soldier was ended by his service to the state. He petitioned the Council of State for 'relief,' as he no longer dared reside 'beyond the seas.'[141]

During March 1651, Parliament and the Council spent much time discussing the traitorous activities of Lord Craven. Aware that the only accusation that could be made against him was that he had remained a loyal friend and supporter of the exiled royal family, on 4 March 1651 they reviewed their sequestration policy. The Calendar for the date shows:

> Upon perusal of the deposition touching
> Lord Craven, presented to the Council for
> the Commissioners of Sequestration ...
> wherein they mention that they had given

orders for seizing and securing his estate,
but doubt that Parliament has made it a
matter of sequestration for any person
living beyond the sea to hold correspondence with or to repair to the King of
Scots, when he was beyond the seas, ...
[they] desire Parliament to give directions
for expediting of justice in such cases.[142]

Three days later the council reported to the Committee for
Sequestration that, concerning the matter of Lord Craven,
Parliament had created new resolutions and 'caused them to be
speedily put in execution, and signify us what you do.'[143]

Shortly thereafter Parliament laid claim to the estate by
charging that Craven had violated the Declaration of August 1649.
According to the Declaration, anyone who betrayed Parliament in
Ireland or assisted Charles II was suspect of treason and in jeopardy of composition or sequestration.[144]

Craven objected, stating that he had given pecuniary and
not vituperative aid. A summons dated 3 July 1651 commanded
Craven to appear before them 'to make answer to all such matters
as should be objected against him in behalf of the Commonwealth
of England.' Ironically, the hearing that Craven ignored was set for
the third of September, the day that the King of Scotland and his
armies were irreversibly defeated by the Commonwealth at
Worcester. During the early months of 1652, the Council had
commented that the greater quantity of oak trees belonging to
Craven in Causham Park in Reading were nicely fit for the navy,
yet they should not be used until further orders were issued. On
11 June they moved to sell Craven's estate, as the resources and
finances would benefit the navy, which was engaged in a costly war
with England's mercantile enemy, Holland. In August 1652,
Parliament passed an act to confiscate Craven's property; and
although he continued to protest their decision, his estates were
not reinstated until 1660.[145]

Throughout his ordeal, Craven was not without his own
loyal supporters. In England and from abroad, they protested
Parliament's decision. First they replied to the charge against
Craven by declaring that, as 'the said Lord was an inhabitant and
sworn servant to that state (the Netherlands) [he was] ... not to be
condemned by the Parliament for his courtesies and duties (as he

calls it) toward their Lordship.'[146] Naturally, this presumption infuriated Parliament. Next, his supporters reminded Parliament how the Declaration of August 1649 specified that the Commonwealth had the right only to punish those who had opposed them in their late struggle with the Irish. They pointed out that this was not the case with Craven. And, of course, they said that the only provable charge was that he had been seen in the king's company in Holland.

Most significantly, perhaps, Craven's followers raised questions about the credibility of the agents upon whose testimonies the state had built its case. In particular, they protested that Falconer's account, which had been instrumental to Parliament's decision, was perjurious. They produced witnesses who disproved what Falconer had said. One witness even produced a copy of the original petition written in Falconer's hand. It did not include the words 'barbarous and inhuman.' After much instigation by Craven's friends, Falconer was indicted for perjury by a grand jury and then tried 'in the presence of as great an appearance as hath been seen at any trial in the courts of Westminster.' After five hours of deliberation on 20 May 1652, he was found 'guilty of corrupt, willful, false and malicious perjury' in his testimony against Craven.[147] However, the decision to confiscate Craven's property, estimated to be worth 12,000 pounds per year, stood.

When Bishop testified at Falconer's trial, he attacked the characters of those who swore that his agent had lied. On both sides there was much of what rhetoricians call an argument *ad hominem*, an appeal that sidesteps issues by shifting the content of the discussion to a personal attack, a method of arguing that was frequently used in the seventeenth century. Consequently, the question of the accuracy and credibility of the state's witnesses, in addition to the validity of the charges against Craven, prompted the writing of several tracts. The pro-Craven tracts raised questions about the state's case and discounted the charges brought against Craven. Bishop too was criticized for his part in this case. An anonymous tract entitled *A Reply to a Certain Pamphlet Written by An Unknowing and Unknown Author* attacked the conduct of Bishop and the Committee for Examinations on grounds similar to those reasoned by Craven's friends.

A major attack on Bishop's conduct in the Craven case was launched by the Presbyterian minister from Bristol, Ralph Farmer. Before the wars Farmer had lost an election to the Common

Council in Bristol, which the king, perhaps on the behalf of Farmer's friend the Earl of Berkshire, sought to have reversed.[148] Farmer's attack, it should be noted, was written in 1657, several years after the royalist case, at a time when he was raking Bishop's past in an effort to discredit his Quakerism. Thus, while we must consider Farmer's accusations, we must also keep in mind that his comments are weakened by the distance of time and shaded by religious and political bias. Farmer considered Bishop to be a cunning, vindictive bureaucrat who would readily sacrifice fairness for a chance to trap a suspected traitor. In a recent article Bishop is credited with the authorship of the 1653 tract, *The Lord Craven's Case As to the Confiscation and Sale of His Estate by Judgment of Parliament.*[149] In the tract Bishop defended his actions on behalf of the Committee for Examinations, while pointing to the flaws in Falconer's perjury trial. Bishop lent Farmer a copy of *The Lord Craven's Case* to guarantee that Farmer would accurately represent his actions as a Commonwealth official in their debate.

This tacit admission to the authoring of *The Lord Craven's Case* surfaced again in Bishop's 1658 tract, *A Rejoinder Consisting of Two Parts.* Here, as would be expected, Bishop defended his actions and those of his agents, citing his resignation as one of the contractors of Lord Craven's estate as an example of his concern for honest testimony. Countering Farmer's accusations, he flatly denied bribing or forcing Falconer to falsify his statement, or adding any lines of his own to the statement. In particular, he defended the credibility of Falconer, whose harsh treatment in jail cost him his life.[150]

He also asserted that he had first met Falconer 'when he was brought to me to give an account of what designed he knew to be hatched against the ... safety of the Commonwealth ... particularly in Norfolk.'[151] Bishop defended the use of harsh penalties for enemies of the state like Craven because the Commonwealth was fearful of presently being dragged into another war. While evidence was being heard against Craven, Bishop's agents were reporting intelligence of the Scottish army, which, bound by the terms of the Treaty of Breda, was making plans for an attack on England.[152] Even in later years, when Bishop was clearly disenchanted with the faltering Protectorate, he continued to defend the state's position in the Craven case.

During the Craven hearings and the investigation of plots in Norfolk, Bishop was communicating another threat to Cromwell:

the division and indecision in the Commonwealth that would deprive it of the internal strength it needed to overcome the external dangers. In a 14 January 1651 letter to Cromwell, Bishop, speaking for himself and on the behalf of Major-General Harrison, expressed concern over the false sense of security at Whitehall since the Norfolk situation. The outbreak of a new insurrection was a real possibility, and with little loyalty to count on in the country, Bishop implored Cromwell to secure a mandate for the expiring militia.[153]

In this letter Bishop also lectured Cromwell for the first of many times about the imminent visitation of an angry God. He also bemoaned the absence of justice and righteousness amongst those in power. One of the main concerns was the restaffing of the Council of State. With the present Council about to expire, Bishop encouraged Cromwell 'to press the Parliament to caution there.' He then boldly warned Cromwell about the rumored dismissal of the current Council president, the High Court Justice John Bradshaw. Bishop learned that Bradshaw was out of favor with Cromwell. In the interest of the Commonwealth, he recommended Bradshaw's honest and noble service.

> I trust the Lord doth give you wisdom to discern such things but this I presume I may say safely that he hath a plain and upright heart, full of courage and nobleness for justice and the Commonwealth, and is so elaborate that whoever succeeds him, the Commonwealth will find a great miss of him.[154]

Four days later, after a brief apology for speaking so boldly, Bishop delivered intelligence of plans for a royalist invasion. Yet once again he revealed his fear for the future of the godly Commonwealth that 'hath the clouds darkening over it.' He wished Cromwell good fortune in the expected troubles from Scotland, but then immediately appended an appeal that 'the Lord guide you and direct you that you may not only lead your forces to the best advantage in that country, but contribute your help to the affairs of this nation, where your spirits and advice is much wanted.'[155] Soon, newly discovered evidence would confirm these forebodings and fan the fears of those in power.

Deare Mr: Winslow:

The Com: for Examinacons haue mett
seen the order made by you upon their Lre.
concerninge Mr Rockett, I tooke it not well that
you should reside what they desired of you (wch.
was not contrary to yr rules) and to referr their
Lre. to the consideration of they knowe not whor
in the Countrey, and to the persons that haue done
Mr Rockett all this Injury. If you peruse the
Lre. I beleiue you will find that in case those
that questioned him after that manner had not
before they they proceeded sufficient matter of
proofe as to delinquency against him, besides wt
hee was questioned for by the Councell, whoe haue
not yet done with him, that you order a present di=
liuery of what was taken from him; you send the
Lre. of yt Councell, and the whole busines to those
that haue done it to Iudge. Pray sr let us
put a difference once betweez repentinge men &
those that goe astray and will not hearken to a
returne, this beinge the only lost sheepe of the
whole tribe that hath returned. I am

Whitehall July 15th
1651

Yor very friend & servt
Geo: Bishope.

*A copy of one of the numerous letters written by George Bishop as Secretary
to the Committee for Examinations. Written to Edward Winslow, it shows
Bishop in disagreement with his superiors at Whitehall.*

The above is Cown copyright reference SP 23/114. It is reproduced by courtesy
of the Controller of Her Majesty's Stationery Office.

CHAPTER THREE

Jerusalem's Impedimenta: Stumbling Blocks Old and New

EARLY 1651 WAS an unusually tense time. Throughout England there were rumors of impending arrests and other measures of control on the part of the state. In March, with the Commonwealth threatened by an invasion from Scotland and with conspiracies afoot at home, Harrison apprehended Thomas Coke, son of Charles I's former secretary in the Strand. As suspected, Coke had returned to England from Holland to continue negotiations with the London Presbyterians, and to help coordinate the local conspiracies that were brewing in the provinces. Underdown has commented that his was one of two arrests that ruined the royalists' chance for an effective uprising and led to dependence on the Scots.[156]

Papers found in Coke's pocket revealed royalist and Presbyterian designs and added substance to Bishop's fear concerning the conspiracy in which Newcastle was a leading figure. In an effort to save his life, Coke disclosed the nature of military and religious networks in existence to return the king. The state learned that there was a major conspiracy among members of the exiled court, the City of London, and certain Presbyterian ministers, including the old enemy of religious toleration, Christopher Love. These ministers were in touch with colleagues in Leicester and Northampton. It was this group, Love in particular, that the Commonwealth used as an example of how traitors would be punished.[157]

His management of intelligence in the case of Love, the Welsh-born Presbyterian minister, illustrates Bishop's intolerance of those who posed a threat to the fragile Commonwealth. Before the war, Love had been a dissenting minister in London who had

40

been denied ordination. Outspoken against Laud in 1640, he had been barred by the Bishop of London from the lectureship of St. Ann's Aldersgate. His rebellious, outspoken nature compelled him to openly criticize the 'errors' in the *Book of Common Prayer*. Love tended to act willfully and without inhibition where circumstances required a more temperate frame of mind. Before the wars, he was arrested, tried, and acquitted at the King's Bench. Love then went to Scotland, where he was welcomed by the presbytery; however, he declined their offer to remain in Scotland.

Love's fortune, if not his outspokenness, changed with the onset of the civil wars and the 1645 establishment of the Presbyterian system. As pastor of St. Ann's, Love's zeal gained him the disfavor of the Independents, who saw him as an enemy of toleration. They disliked and distrusted him. In 1648, they accused him of undermining the negotiations between the Parliamentary commissions and those of the king. He provoked the anger of both sides as his fiery sermons threatened to exacerbate the frenzy that was upon London. Love scorned the king and his party, believing a covenant with them to have the value of a 'loose halter about an ape's neck, which they can put on and off at pleasure.'[158]

Angered by the 1648 exclusion of some Presbyterian members from Parliament, Love's preaching added to the already tense relations between the various religious groups. He rejected any offers to come to agreement with the Independents and sectarians, remarking to the preacher Hugh Peter and Colonel Okey: 'Ye are a company of heretics and schismatics, and the curse of God is on you and will destroy you. I will not have to do with you.'[159] Under the watchful eyes of his Independent enemies, Love's activities were monitored, and before 1651 he had been taken into custody at least once.[160]

Unfortunately for Love, the detained Coke revealed the plot to Scot and Bishop's agents at the time when fear and suspicion ran rampant in England: The Scottish army was moving southward and continued warfare was inevitable. Moreover, it was likely that he would be dealt with harshly, since his old enemies, the religious Independents, were in a favorable position in the Rump Parliament.[161] Parliament was indeed incensed, as Bishop's men discovered that Love and his co-conspirators were in correspondence with the king's friends, who were exiled in France and Holland, and with the Scottish Presbyterians. Agents Harvey and Adams kept

41

Bishop informed of the activities that went on in Love's home, an important base of the operation and clearinghouse for contributions. Eventually Love and other ministers were accused that they 'did traitorously and maliciously incite, aid and assist the Scots, ... foreigners and strangers to invade the Commonwealth of England, and [that they] adhered to the forces of the enemy raised against the Parliament and Commonwealth aforesaid and keepers of the liberties of England.'[162] At Love's trial, Adam's first-hand information was among the most incriminating evidence against him.

Love wrote several petitions to Parliament throughout his ordeal. Yet he may have been his own worst enemy, as his statements strongly suggested his guilt. Throughout the lengthy and well-attended trial, Love held fast to the notion that he did 'nothing out of animosity or stoutness, but only for conscience.'[163] Despite strong public opinion and an outpouring of favorable tracts, Love and his fellow ministers were found guilty of high treason by the High Court of Justice. To no avail, Love appealed on the technicality that his actions predated the March 1650 act that ordained the new court. After a month's reprieve, he was executed in August 1651, less than one month before the Battle of Worcester.

At Whitehall, Bishop expressed a concern for the safety of the new Commonwealth. 'Through the finger of God,' he said, 'these designs [had been brought] into light ... [and] had sealed the case against Love.'[164] Working closely with Harrison, Bishop expressed their joint sentiment that it was the anti-Christ who had forced these traitors to 'hinder the safety of the Commonwealth.'[165] Clearly, then, Love had to be dealt with harshly in recompense for 'the providence of God in the field and at home, the blood, the costs and miseries of war.'[166] Vane, John Milton, and other radicals also believed that Love and his brethren deserved severe punishment, as they had disregarded the lawful magistracy of the Commonwealth. Bishop and his associates were imbued with a sense of obligation to subdue God's enemies or to face some form of punishment. During the seventeenth century, disregarding the will of providence, as one historian has noted, was considered 'a fundamental political error.'[167]

Bishop's determination to have Love found guilty and executed caused Ralph Farmer in later years to discredit his piety. According to Farmer, Bishop had acted viciously against Love during the ordeal and, after his execution, 'killed him again' through the slanders that he wrote. In his 1657 tract, *Satan Inthron'd*, Farmer named Bishop as the author of several anti-Love tracts, including *Mr. Love's Case* and *A Short Plea for the Commonwealth*.

In *Satan Inthron'd*, Farmer accused Scot and Bishop of forgery and procedural violations. Bishop, of course, denied that he or any member of the Committee for Examinations had added six lines to Love's confession or forced him to sign a confession. According to Bishop, all discrepancies had been removed to Love's satisfaction, and he explained that it was standard procedure for an accused traitor to be denied a copy of his confession. Contrary to Farmer's accusations, in his own confession to the restored royalists in 1660, Scot stated that he had interceded in 1651 on Love's behalf.[168]

Joseph Martin has pointed out how the tracts published in response to the Love trial, except those written by Love himself, were all anonymous. Yet Bishop's authorship is suggested by the spirit and wording of *A Short Plea for the Commonwealth Discovering the Treasonable Practices of Mr. Christopher Love*. When Bishop responded to Farmer's accusations of cruelty and dishonesty, he did not deny authorship of *A Short Plea*, as he did with another tract, *Mr. Love's Case*.

Upon examination, the line of reasoning in *A Short Plea* closely resembles that in Bishop's July 1651 letter on the subject. What is more significant is the fact that much of the wording is identical. Written in July 1651, the month during which Love had a reprieve, Bishop again reasoned that, as God had generously manifested his providence on the field, and as the English people had suffered miserably during the wars, the state had an obligation to deal harshly with traitors. The imminence of a royalist attack on England, and the havoc that would follow, were further justification for Love's execution. At all costs the Commonwealth's safety and well-being must be secured.[169]

In *Satan Inthron'd*, Farmer insisted that Scot and Bishop had been unnecessarily heavy-handed in the Love case. They claimed that, 'until ... some others were dealt with as Love was, it would never be well.'[170] Yet through Bishop's response to this accusation, we gain insight into his thinking. His position in the Love case, it should be noted, bears a close resemblance to the one he took at Putney on the question of bringing the king to justice. In *A Rejoinder*, Bishop explained that vigilance against the accused was in actuality a continuation of the army's work against the ungodly. Their blood was needed to secure the delicate safety of the pre-Worcester Commonwealth. Patricia Crawford has explained the concept of 'blood guilt' as a way of divesting royalty of its divine nature by appropriating the ancient belief in shedding the blood of those who killed the righteous.[171] According to Bishop, the state needed to continue the work the army had begun. In many ways Love's execution was a justification for that of Charles I. He wrote:

> And this I say to the army, either lay down
> the cause and confess yourselves guilty of
> all the blood spilt in the war, or let that be
> reproved as it deserves, which thus spits
> in the face of it, and of you, and of those
> who acted with you, and of their author-
> ity and justice from whence you received
> your commission.[172]

Moreover, Bishop charged Love and the other accused ministers of thirsting after the blood of the Commonwealth. The ministers' evil intentions were manifested in their support of the Scots in recent battles. Their greatest treason was

> the assuming unto themselves a supreme
> power within the jurisdiction of the
> Commonwealth to give commission and
> instructions to diverse persons, authoriz-
> ing them to treat with a foreign state and
> the proclaimed enemy of the
> Commonwealth, Charles Stuart, King of
> Scots for the setting of him by force of
> arms into the throne of England.[173]

Bishop reasoned that Love had placed the Covenant above the safety of the Commonwealth, sabotaging the army's efforts in its campaign against the rebels. If the plotters had been success-ful in their efforts, there would have been two supreme powers— Parliament and the king—each claiming legal authority. There would have been more bloodshed and more turmoil in the already war-weary England. Thus Bishop maintained that it was more judicious to secure the safety of the vulnerable nation than to spare the life of one traitorous Englishman. Hopefully, the execution of

Love by the High Court would deter other enemies of the godly Commonwealth from committing similar mistakes. Bishop asserted that, to establish the Commonwealth and secure peace, the Court had 'to curb and extirpate the licentiuosness of the clergy in what concerns the affairs of the state, likewise to let them know at what rate they shall bury their treasons.'[174]

Love's trial and death came at a time of political crisis. According to Worden, Love's case symbolizes the tensions among the King's enemies created by the unresolvable differences concerning reform.[175] The fear that Love provoked, he notes, was sharpened by the fact that, 'on the day … [he] went to the block, Charles II's Scottish army, having marched south through England, was encamping at Worcester.'[176]

The most dramatic demonstration of the effectiveness of Scot and Bishop's intelligence operation was the role it played in Cromwell's final military victory at Worcester in September 1651. Behind the 'crowning mercy,' as Cromwell termed this triumph, lay a number of well-directed arrests by Bishop's agents in the months that preceded Worcester.[177] As late as mid-August 1651, the Council of State expressed concern that the enemy seemed to have the advantage. On August 24 they sent Lambert and Harrison a copy of a report on the enemy's progress that had been written by one of Bishop's men. It provoked the response that 'these quick marches of the enemy, and the advantage which he has met with, we look upon as adding reputation to him, and putting suffering upon our friends where they come, and this obliges us all to our quickest resolutions and endeavors, for prevention of what further harm we may.'[178] As the Scottish army marched south, Bishop's men mixed with them to gain intelligence. Writing from the army's headquarters near Worcester, Robert Stapylton reported intelligence to Bishop. It was immediately evident that their victory at Worcester 'was the beginning of their [enemy's] fall before the appearance of the Lord Jesus … [and] this seems to be the setting of that young king's glory.' Stapylton informed Bishop of how Fleetwood's brigade 'with much courage and resolution' met the king's forces as each side advanced from opposing sides of the Severn River. As the Lord saw fit, Stapylton reported, the enemy underestimated the strength of the Commonwealth's forces. Making 'a very bad salley,' the king's army was forced to retreat, leaving behind ammunition that would be much needed should the brigade that was dispatched to catch up with them do so. It was immediately clear that this was 'a great victory' from which the defeated forces would never recover.[179]

Yet any relief Bishop may have felt by the royalist defeat was eclipsed by concern that his associates were mishandling their godly mandate. As in the affair of the Forest of Dean some four years earlier, Bishop again found the Commonwealth's servants mismanaging public affairs. On September 23 he wrote to Edward Winslow, the former governor of New Plymouth Colony, who had been made a member of the Committee for Sequestration and Advancement of Money and for Compounding with Delinquents upon his return to England. The following letter provides clear insight into Bishop's disillusionment with the Committee and with the Council of State. Bishop took Winslow to task regarding the mismanagement of the sequestration proceedings against the Nottinghamshire minister John Rockett. The letter confirms the animosity that we are told former royalists, neutrals, and Parliamentarians alike had for the sequestration committees.[180] Yet as the lengthy excerpt demonstrates, it is a unique example, as the accusation of inequity and rapine was made by one of the committee's own associates. Bishop wrote the following letter:

> My dear friend,
>
> I am sorry that such things as the matter enclosed should put the Council, yourselves and my particular to that trouble as the nature of them doth import. Tis not only strange but sad to me, that there should be such proceedings as if there were no authority or law in England ... It is a sad thing to see a man's estate secured, deposed, his lands let out, corn threshed, sold and without the deposition of two sufficient witnesses first had ... to have your own written orders to deliver what was secured upon bond to be responsible, to have the Council of State and the Lord President villified and abused by those ministers together with many other particulars mentioned in the enclosed and all

46

to an honest man, whom God hath made sensible of his failings; one who is and whom the Council had signified to you to be under their Examination and to whom the state had and will show mercy: There being nothing remitted to you from them to proceed to sequestrations, against whom there is nothing deposed who was not apprehended by any warrant ... I hope you will at length put an end to this business with such tenderness and justice as becomes you to the honest man and the Council and your trusts. Certainly God is angry at these things and men are not pleased. Let the state be esteemed a little higher.... I write not to you as if you were guilty of these things, for I know you, your faithfulness and conscience, but being grieved in spirit that such things should be done I have manifested it to you, and am...

Your faithful friend and servant,

George Bishop[181]

Bishop continued as a loyal civil servant of the state, with Scot as his immediate superior, but from 1652 it became evident that his intelligence activities were being curtailed. In June the Council ordered that he make 'an extract of intelligence from letters come to his hands and deliver it to Mr. Thurloe.'[182] At this time Thurloe's involvement in intelligence was increasing, as was his influence with the Council of State.

With the threat of royalist rising at home minimized after Worcester, Bishop began to involve himself in foreign intelligence. During the first Dutch War in 1652, he gathered reports from agents in Holland and forwarded them to the MP Bulstrode Whitelocke. He kept Whitelocke posted on the Dutch Republic's difficulties in continuing the war with England, while it was confronting pressure at home to return the Prince of Orange as Stadtholder. The Dutch were facing the threat of unrest and increasing difficulty in financing the unpopular war. In part, the war had been instigated by the passage of the 1650 English Act of Navigation, which restricted foreign vessels from trading with England. A supporter of the Act of Navigation, the Bristol native found the mercantile republic to be a tenacious enemy, writing to Whitelocke 13 September 1652, outraged that 'they bend not to submit to the hand of God or to this Commonwealth.'[183]

Yet there was another concern that worried Bishop. He implored Whitelocke to return to London, as 'the fundamental affairs of this state are on foot and the concern thereof into consideration in immediate junctive I think you have not a greater. The Parliament at home and the navy abroad and the concern of peace and war and your settlement are deeply engaged.'[184]

Until Worcester, the army and Parliament were preoccupied with the Commonwealth's safety. After 1651, it would seem that Parliament had the opportunity to effect the political and religious reforms for which they had gone to war. Yet during the months before Cromwell dissolved the Rump, it had become increasingly evident that they would not legislate reform. Recently, historian Derek Hirst has assessed the situation, commenting that:

> The dashing of the Hale Commission for law reform underlined the message of the Rump's legislative records, which showed only one-third as many public bills passed in 1652 as in 1649. The pressure of business on a weary legislature which was also a wartime executive explains much; furthermore, leading reformers were gone, Ireton dead in Ireland in 1651, Vane immersed in his navy work. But radicals took more notice of the members' concern for their own interests.[185]

To the dismay of Cromwell and the army, the members of this sparse, inactive body were preventing their own dissolution. Cromwell became enraged when he learned that the House was preparing a bill to prolong their existence. In September 1652 Bishop explained the situation to Whitelocke and wrote that 'the committee for the bill for a new representative goes on: the house have ordered themselves to be called [on] November 3rd ... [yet there is] hardly enough now to make a house, some afternoons not enough to make a council.'[186]

Cromwell also spoke to Whitelocke concerning the Rump and criticized their 'delays of business, and designs to perpetuate themselves, and to continue the power in their own hands.'[187] Cromwell also sought Whitelocke's advice on a related issue: whether or not 'a man could take it upon himself to be king.'[188] Whitelocke responded that 'their friends' had decided upon a free state instead of a monarchy after the late wars. He reasoned that, if the nation were now confronted with the choice of a free state or a monarchy, Cromwell would alienate his supporters. Sadly, the nation would be faced with a Stuart restoration.[189]

A month earlier, Bishop too had discussed the Rump and religious reform with Cromwell. Concerning Parliament's failure to create a settlement that would insure liberty of conscience, Cromwell told Bishop:

> Whatever men think and say of me, yet the end will make it appear that I have nothing in mine eye but the glory of God and the good of these nations: And if in mine old age, through my folly, I shall spill all these mercies on the ground the Lord hath shown me know this, God will not bless me.[190]

In 1659, while petitioning for the abolition of tithes and the mitigation of Quaker suffering, Bishop would tell the army and the restored Rump Parliament of his opposition to Cromwell's April 1653 'interruption.' He would report that he had 'observed the workings in him [Cromwell] (and he knew it) that misled you [the army] from Worcester fight to that time [April 1653].'[191] Bishop apparently knew that there was talk in London of making Cromwell king, and probably discussed the matter with Whitelocke. Opposed to such a notion, Bishop maintained that he had attempted to 'put checks to his [Cromwell's] career in that attempt ... and signified it to some members of Parliament whom I could trust, and proposed a plain way for the prevention thereof.'[192]

In the spring of 1653, the army was pressuring Cromwell to dissolve the Rump, which had been 'clinging to authority for the sake of the corrupt profits that power put in their grasp.'[193] Both Cromwell and the army believed that Parliament was disregarding godly interests. For example, the House had refused to renew the

49

reformist Commission for the Propagation of the Gospel in Wales. Formed in 1650, the Commission was popular with radical ministers and was under the direction of Bishop's associate, Thomas Harrison. After three years, the Rump declined to renew the Commission, giving the appearance that they were frustrating religious reform. Already under pressure to dissolve Parliament, Cromwell ordered Harrison to do so when he learned that the House was about to vote on the self-perpetuating Bill for a New Representative.[194]

On 4 July 1653, a new Parliament convened. It was chosen largely by the Council of Officers of the Army. For the radical sectaries, this Parliament was the instrument of providence that would transform England into the New Jerusalem. Through legislation, it was hoped that they would bring about a political, legal, and religious settlement that would purge the Commonwealth of the ambiguities and corruption that had followed the civil wars. The purified church and state would be pleasing to God and to man. When the Nominated Parliament first met, Cromwell himself commented: 'Indeed I think something is at the door: we are at the threshold and therefore it becomes us to lift up our heads and encourage ourselves in the Lord ... we are on the edge of promises and prophecies.'[195]

In actuality, however, this Parliament was plagued by conflicting viewpoints concerning law reform, tithes, the hiring of the ministry, and the ownership of parish livings. As with the Rump, members quit or neglected to attend. In December 1653 a core of moderate members under the leadership of Maj.-Gen. Lambert abdicated their authority to the army, which in turn cleared the House of the remaining radical members.[196]

Bishop, who had opposed the decision to dissolve the Rump, nevertheless accepted the authority of the nominated MPs and recognized their attempts to legislate the much-needed reforms.[197] Yet in terms of his own political career, what might have been a summer of promise was quickly becoming an autumn of discontent. Although Bishop may have been enchanted by Cromwell's July speech, the fact remained that he was out of favor with Cromwell, too.[198] Wherever he looked, whether at the Committee for Composition, the Council, or the Lord General, Bishop watched corruption replace reform and indecision harden into impasse.

In July 1653, Bishop was discharged from 'intermeddling in foreign affairs.'[199] The Council, in light of the debts incurred by the Dutch War, had reordered their priorities and questioned the costly expenses for which Bishop sought reimbursement. For whatever reasons, the Council had been steadily diminishing Bishop's responsibilities, while Thurloe was quickly becoming the central figure in foreign and domestic intelligence. As Thurloe's influence with Cromwell waxed, that of Scot and Bishop waned.

In February 1653, the Council had ordered a correspondent to discontinue delivering intelligence to Bishop and henceforth to forward all dispatches to Scot.[200] At this time Bishop was among those who remained in favor of the Dutch War, while Cromwell and some members of the Council had become disinterested in continuing with what was becoming a disaster to the trading interests, navy, and treasury. There was a strong representation of members who shared Cromwell's call for peace in the new Council of State that was elected in November 1652. Like earlier Councils, this one appointed its own committees. They delayed the reappointment of the Committee for Examinations. It was under their direction that Bishop's duties at Whitehall were curtailed and that his attitude towards the government became increasingly critical.[201]

On 6 September 1653, Bishop wrote to the Council requesting a leave from his duties and a settlement of his outstanding accounts. It is the fullest extant account of Bishop's political disillusionment. It reads:

I continued in course from Council to Council ... the Committee leaving the whole management of intelligence and the disbursements thereof to me, and never interfered, although I often desired it, they having more experience therein; at the end of every year Council appointed a Committee to receive my accounts, which were always passed without hesitation. Council not reviving that Committee last December, I went on as before and presented what intelligence came to hand to Council, who gave me a warrant for

51

payment of my disbursements, and although I petitioned for their discharge, I did not obtain it. Upon the late change, I also continued, although Mr. Scot ceased to supply his intelligence, and out of respect to all, I waited on the Lord General with what I had received as to the state of affairs in Holland, and other things of consequence to the ending of the war and from time to time gave his Excellency and Council what I received from my agents. I acquainted his Lordship with the chargeableness of my employment, and that for several months I had not received any money, and desired a settlement, which he often promised ... I never intended from the first day of my coming hither to set up a tabernacle, but have constantly pressed as the affairs of the Commonwealth would permit to be dismissed, I having here little advantage except the loss of my calling, the prejudice of my estate, the wearying of my body, breaking of my health, neglect of my family, and encountering temptations of all sorts [and] prejudices ... hatreds, malice and abuses which the faithful discharge of my duty had exposed me to, in no small measure ... and the keeping of 600 pounds and sometimes 1000 pounds always ready by me of my own money to carry on my correspondence when Council had no money in their treasury ... As to the continuance of my employment, I am not yet discharged from the part which relates to home-bred treasons and conspiracies, though I supposed little of that is expected from me in that regard ... I desire your pleasure as to my full discharge, and as I have received mercy from the Lord to be faithful to the Commonwealth in all its turns and dangers, not serving any man or myself, but in order to the will of the Lord and the common good ... so I shall, through the same goodness, persevere as I have opportunity in my private capacity and retirement.[202]

Thus, at the end of 1653, with the secured Commonwealth about to abdicate its own existence; with radicals disturbed over the absence of political and religious reforms; and with critics of Cromwell, like Scot, Harrison, and Whitelocke out of favor, Bishop sought retirement from London politics. Eventually the Council, elected in November 1653, expressed an interest in employing him to gather intelligence, perhaps as a first move toward reinstating the intelligence privileges he had formerly enjoyed.

But on 10 November 1653, Bishop wrote to Whitelocke, who was serving as Ambassador at the Swedish Court. He explained, 'I am putting foot in stirrup for Bristol where I hope to live retired ... and in a private condition serve the public as I am able, for I walk on principles.'[203]

Thus, shortly after November 1653 a disenchanted Bishop left London and returned to Bristol. Upon his arrival, he was met by friends and neighbors who had joined the radical sects. They had been moved by the spirit of the Lord to spread the message of truth to those with 'principles' who were prepared to embrace it.

CHAPTER FOUR

Disenchanted Radical
Turns Quaker

AFTER MORE THAN three years of living and working among the Commonwealth's servants, Bishop returned to Bristol and found the royalist supporters in charge of city politics.[204] For the most part these were the same rich merchants who had run the city before the wars.[205] The Presbyterian and royalist sympathizers who controlled the city corporation were referred to collectively as the 'royalist party' by Bishop and his army, Independent, and sectarian associates. As in other parts of England, there was a lack of enthusiasm in Bristol for the new order. Often little was done when Whitehall's policies failed to be carried out in the provinces. Underdown has found that 'plundering soldiers, quartering, impressment, committee misgovernment' all converged between 1646 and 1648 to produce a general mood of alienation from Parliament and its local institutions.[206] Hence for Bishop it must have not been surprising that the Bristolians who had sided with the king in the late wars were openly serving as aldermen and councilmen and were holding some of the highest posts in the city.

The 'royalist party's' influence was so conspicuous that the commander of the garrison in the city, Gov. Adrian Scrope, wrote to Cromwell and asked him to 'put a check on the enemies of God who now exceedingly insult and think to carry all before them.'[207] As might be expected, the Bristol magistrates resented Bishop's army associates, in particular Scrope and Capts. Beale and Watson, who commanded the garrison. To the merchant magistrates of Bristol, the army was surely a reminder of the strife that had forced them to subordinate matters of business to those of war.

Moreover, the conservative groups in the city, and the Presbyterian oligarchy who, according to Cole, controlled the post-war City Council, were agitated that many soldiers practiced or embraced the religious innovations of the radical sectaries.[208] Radicals, Independents and sectaries, known collectively as the 'godly party,' had been an annoying presence in Bristol since at least 1641, when Bishop's friend Dennis Hollister, a grocer of some wealth and influence in the city, was accused of holding a conventicle at his home.[209]

During and after the wars, Hollister and Bishop had a close association with Maj.-Gen. Thomas Harrison. Harrison was among the first who sought to bring Charles Stuart, 'that man of blood,' to justice. Distrustful of the earthly government, Harrison and his fellow Fifth Monarchists awaited Christ's second coming and the rule of the saints.[210] Presbyterian minister Ralph Farmer charged that

> This Hollister and some of his adherents (under the name and notion of the godly and well-affected party) [was] much encouraged by the interest and favor he had with a Major-General [Harrison], a person at that time eminent and of great power ... [and] also by the advantage and assistance of George Bishop, residing at Whitehall, who was then a man of some credit.[211]

Bishop's work at Whitehall had earned him the animosity of some Presbyterian ministers and their supporters on the City Council. In 1651 he had gathered information concerning dangerous ministers in Bristol and presented the case of the Rev. Constant Jessop to the Council of State. The safety of the government, Bishop reported, was jeopardized by an inflammatory sermon Jessop had preached at the Bristol parish of St. Nicholas, where he was pastor. Through Jessop's own admission, the Council of State learned that the sermon was preached 'at the choice of the mayor.' Regarding the sermon's content as dangerous, they deprived Jessop of his ministry and prohibited him from coming within ten miles of Bristol. In May 1654, however, after petitioning the protector, Jessop had the order reversed and resumed his preaching.[212] Hence, upon his return from Whitehall, Bishop was disappointed to find that it was the army and the sectaries, not the Presbyterian ministers, who were scorned and distrusted by the local authorities.

Bishop sought to address this lack of political and religious reform in Bristol, and what he saw as Cromwell's failure to effect change, through election to the 1654 Parliament. According to Farmer, Bishop voiced his criticism of Cromwell, contending that: 'We must choose Parliament men as should hold my lord protector's nose to the grindstone.'[213] In the July election, he and his cousin Judge John Haggett were supported as candidates by Scrope, Hollister, and other members of the 'godly party.' Unsuccessful in the election, Bishop and Haggett were defeated by Robert Aldworth, a distant relation of Bishop's; and Miles Jackson, who prior to the city's retaking of Bristol had lent Charles I financial support and signed the protestation against the Earl of Essex that denounced any aiding, supporting, or communicating with the enemies.[214] As the election results demonstrated, the preservation of the city's interest and traditional leadership, not innovation, would prevail in Bristol.

The godly party was outraged over the election's results, and it is possible that Bishop organized the protest that followed. The Council of State received complaints that the election results were invalid since the royalist party had improperly influenced the proceedings. Several petitions concerning the election's unfairness were sent to the Council, along with supporting documentation that included lists of those who voted on either side.[215]

In a sworn deposition, one Nicholas Halloway, a Bristol merchant, related how, 'when sheriffs were taking the pole between Mr. Alderman Miles Jackson and Mr. Haggett for the second burgess, Capt. George Bishop came up in the [Guild] Hall with soldiers armed and protested against the proceedings of the sheriffs.[216] Sacks found that a number of Bishop's supporters withheld their votes because they believed their opponents' supporters lack of eligibility had compromised the election's legality.[217]

One petition with ninety-five signatures reported to Cromwell and the Council the conditions under which Bishop and Haggett lost the election. It explained how some in Bristol who were 'friends to Parliament' had expected the election to run in accordance with the Instrument of Government, excluding those from participating 'who had favored the late king.' The city's sheriffs, with assurances from their own legal advisors, encouraged the royalists to vote, 'promising to bear them out in so doing.' The petitioners contended that the local officials acted in violation of the Instrument, 'carr[ying] on as if there were no Comonwealth or protector.'[218]

Nonetheless, in September, Aldworth and Jackson left Bristol and took their seats in Parliament. Before they left, the city corporation, weary of the radical sectaries and their army supporters, handed them their written 'instructions' to promote 'spreading the gospel in dark places, to settle the maintenance of ministers by tithes.'[219] It seems that the city corporation was dissatisfied with the provisions for religious liberty outlined in the Instrument of Government, the constitution that followed the abdication of the Nominated Parliament and empowered Cromwell as Lord Protector. They wanted their representatives to use their mandate 'to establish order in the church.'[220] As in other locales, the unconventional principles and practices of the radical sectaries were alarming the authorities.

These groups had their distinguishing characteristics, yet they commonly followed what they took to be the early Christian model of a ministry of laypersons who preached to gatherings in the counties through which they passed. These outspoken, often argumentative sectaries met with animosity from the ministers and magistrates in Bristol and indeed throughout much of England. Their rejection of certain time-honored institutions and social conventions—paying tithes, taking oaths, and offering hat honor and deferential language to their superiors—served to provoke much of the hostility they met.[221] In regard to one such group, the Quakers, Secretary of State John Thurloe was warned to 'let order and established government have a high place in your thoughts, and that in church as well as state.'[222] Their disapproval of a paid ministry was viewed as a threat to authority. Order, it was feared, would be replaced by anarchy, as sectaries would next claim to be their own ministers and magistrates.[223] Deploring the outward artifacts of religion, they met for worship in their homes or in open fields. They preached millenarian visions of the imminent rule of Christ and his saints, along with warnings and prophecies that their internal spirit compelled them to deliver.

Bishop would soon join the group of radical sectaries that originated in the north who called themselves the Children of the Light. Commonly called "Quakers" by their detractors, this group's conventions and doctrines were largely shaped by George Fox and James Nayler, both of Puritan ancestry. Fox of Leicestershire was a cobbler's apprentice who had been effectively gathering followers since 1646 as he spread the doctrine of the inner light of Jesus Christ throughout the north and midlands.[224] This notion of religious 'certainty' assures salvation through the reception of an inward, spiritual Christ. In his *Journal*, Fox defined the inner light as 'that which reacheth this witness of God in yourselves.'[225] Nayler, who was married and the father of young children, had been a quartermaster in Lambert's division during the civil wars. Dissatisfied with what he saw as the failure of the Parliamentary cause, he had put aside his private affairs and involved himself in Fox's work.

Fox and Nayler encouraged their followers to worship in silence and to deliver testimonies of truth as they were moved by the Lord. These testimonies were unsolicited warnings of divine retribution, generally directed at 'wayward' ministers. The Quakers were despised by Presbyterians and Independents; and depending on the extension of the interruption, the turmoil it caused, and the congregation's own religious prejudices, they were identified as Ranters, Jesuits, or Anabaptists. The Quakers lived simply and had little use for frivolities. They refused to show deference to social superiors and maintained that, according to the Bible, no man was entitled to receive hat honor or to be addressed with the second person pronoun 'you.' Like other radical sects, the Quakers rejected the system of paying ministers with tithes.

The Quakers sometimes escaped harm or punishment through the intervention of several judges, including Thomas Fell and Bishop's associate from Whitehall, John Bradshaw. After Fox preached at Fell's Westmoreland home, Swarthmore, it became the first center of Quaker operations, and his wife, Margaret Fell, became its first patron. It was at Swarthmore that Quakers from England, Ireland, and Scotland became acquainted, and where they formed a fellowship of shared beliefs and mutual support. Margaret Fell organized the transmission of news and funds to trusted Quakers like Bishop. These local organizers arranged meetings for worship and coordinated affairs in their locales. They also circulated news to what was becoming a large network of brethren.[226]

From early in the movement, the Quakers relied on the printing press to spread ideas and news of their encounters with the authorities. Inexpensive tracts found their way to the counties, where traveling preachers would leave a supply before moving on to their next destination.[227] Traveling in pairs, the preachers visited the counties armed with their convictions and imbued with a concern for group organization. They disseminated news and established local communities of mutual support. Under the leadership of men like Bishop, who were effective organizers and propagandists, the Quakers became remarkably self-reliant. When they met the hostility of the mob or of the authorities, it seemed that their group cohesion, created by the movement's effective leadership, enabled them to confront and endure opposition.

They received food and shelter at their brethren's homes and were remunerated for their expenses through the Kendal fund 'for the service of truth.' Fell, who regularly sheltered Quaker travelers, was among those who developed, supported, and coordinated this fund. With this support, John Audland and Thomas Ayrey visited Bristol in July 1654. Audland returned with his fellow preacher, John Camm, and during their September visit Quakerism was established in Bristol.[228]

Bishop and his friends may have asked the soldiers in Bristol to protect Audland, Ayrey, and Camm because earlier preachers had been harassed by local Presbyterian ministers. For instance, when Morgan Lloyd and the Seeker William Erbury arrived in Bristol to preach, the Rev. Ralph Farmer had locked them out of his parish. It was only after some soldiers intervened that Lloyd and Erbury had been permitted to preach to the congregation. As would happen with the arrival of the Quakers, the early preachers angered the ministers as they exposed their congregations to 'heretical' ideas.[229]

When Audland and Camm arrived they preached to Bristol's Baptist and Independent congregations. Those most receptive to their ideas, however, were the Seekers, a group of radicals with austere conventions who waited in silence for a sign of apostolic truth.[230] With what seems to have been mixed motives, some religious, some political, Governor Scrope offered 'that if the magistrates did put the [Quakers] in prison one day, he would put

59

them out the next.'[231]   Capts. Beale and Watson, along with their wives, were so cordial to the Quaker preachers that, after Audland left Bristol, he wrote to Beale with the familiarity that is characteristic of a respected family friend. Audland reported that 'we met at the fort where the soldiers are. The greatest meeting I ever saw.'[232] Large numbers of Bristolians were drawn to these Quaker meetings, which soon required large, open areas to accommodate all who came.

Who in Bristol became Quakers after the arrival of these preachers? And what influences in postwar Bristol prepared people like Bishop to accept their ideas? As Vann found in his study, Quakers in Bristol were in actuality more prosperous than they had been portrayed in contemporary and literary accounts. There is no evidence that the movement attracted either the downtrodden or vagrants. On the contrary, in Bristol many converts were leading citizens like Bishop. A study of seventeenth-century Bristol Quaker records found:

> About ten percent of heads of families described themselves as merchants, compared with percentages of six in the learned professions [legal, medicine and education], twenty in other branches of commerce and consumption goods twenty in mechanical trades ... and nearly forty percent in the weaving, clothing and allied trades.[233]

Bishop and his neighbor, the Baptist grocer Dennis Hollister, were among the most prominent early Bristol converts. While he sat in the Nominated Parliament, Hollister was allegedly influenced by Quaker ideas. An elder in the Broadmead Baptist Church, the congregation stopped conducting meetings at his home once he began introducing Quaker ideas. Their church records state:

> Mr. Hollister staying in London sucked in some principles of the locust doctrine from a sort of people called Quakers. That when Parliament was dissolved by Oliver, Dennis came home from London with his

60

heart full of discontent and his head full
of poisonous new notions ... And he
began to vent himself ... At one meeting
of the church, after he came down he did
blasphemously say the bible was the
plague of England. From that time the
church would meet no more at his
house.[234]

Bishop was also exposed to Quaker and other radical ideas
during his years in London. At Putney, the radicals had offered
their version of church reform and had argued for liberty of
conscience as a fundamental right. Bishop's associate on the
Committee for Examinations, Maj.-Gen. Harrison, enthusiastically
preached the Fifth Monarchist idea that Christ would rule the earth
for a thousand years with the assistance of the 'godly saints.' Like
the early Quakers, the Fifth Monarchists quoted frequently from
the Book of Daniel and from the Revelation of St. John the Divine.
Thus Harrison may have influenced the millenarian and apocalyptic thought that pervaded the warnings and prophecies that Bishop
wrote as a Quaker. When the survival of sectarian religion looked
bleak shortly after the Restoration, Bishop extended encouragement
to the Fifth Monarchists and reminded them that 'the way is easy
... and you know it ... For there is no other name given under heaven
by which we can be saved than by Christ the light ... [to] which John
bore testimony ... and he saith that the light shineth in darkness.'[235]
Among his close associates were Henry Vane Jr and Judge John
Bradshaw, who had a reputation of befriending Quakers who
encountered difficulties with the law.[236]

Sometime around October 1654 George and Elizabeth
Bishop began their association with the Quaker community. We
do not have an exact date or account of George Bishop's decision
to become a Quaker, yet we know that, during Edward Burrough
and Francis Howgill's October 1654 visit to Bristol, Bishop hosted
Quaker meetings at his Corn Street home, 'a large house with large
rooms.'[237] Bishop described the longing for spiritual fulfillment
that had preceded the arrival of the Quaker preachers in Bristol.
He wrote:

People of God in and about the city of
Bristol (as in divers other parts of this

nation), having a long time wandered from mountain to hill, from one form to another, [were] seeking rest, but finding none and ... receiving no satisfaction from the forms in which they walked and wherein they did abide.[238]

During the chaos of the postwar years the traditions and institutions that had defined the order of daily life had disappeared or been redefined. The appearance of new political institutions and religious innovations created a population who longed for a sense of stability. In Bishop's case, although it was his allies who initiated the postwar legislation, he would still experience the feeling of anxiety that accompanies war and political change. Thus we must review the circumstances that preceded Bishop's conversion to Quakerism during late 1654 or 1655. His decision to convert must be considered in the context of his various political disappointments in Bristol and London, his resignation at Whitehall and his continued interest in the affairs of the city corporation that had become hostile to him and his associates.

After more than three years of employment in London, working among political and religious radicals who had a voice in political affairs, Bishop returned to Bristol, where the ministers and magistrates were seeking a conservative religious policy. Royalist sympathizers controlled civic affairs; and according to the protests sent to the Council of State in response to the July 1654 Parliamentary election, they were circumventing policy that had prohibited their participation.

Despite the honor that was bestowed on Bishop by the Merchant Venturers in 1651, he was neither appointed to a post in the city government nor given any gesture of the magistrates' good will upon his return from London. Instead, it happened that Presbyterian ministers, a group whom he and his Whitehall colleagues had found hostile to the Commonwealth, were given reprieves for past infractions and the opportunity to resume their positions. No longer in active military service, he was still known as 'Captain' Bishop, an identification that would gain the animosity of the authorities, who resented the army's presence in the city. His association with Bradshaw, Harrison, Scot, and other radicals in London, and with Hollister and the sectaries in Bristol, surely worked against any hope he had for a future in local affairs.

It seems reasonable that Bishop needed a new center for his existence. And in a deeply religious century where spiritual and political matters were indistinguishable, sectarian religion was a logical outlet for those who felt a sense of disenchantment or alienation. Like the cases of conversion that William James documented, Bishop's conversion was associated with crisis, disillusionment, and a shift in personal energy.[239] In Quakerism he apparently found the inward stability that compensated for the external disunity over which he had no control.

During 1655, in his first Quaker tract, Bishop would assert that 'the principle of Light which we witness in measure, leads us out of wars, strife, envy, debate or doing evil to any ... but that all might come to the knowledge of truth ... vengeance we leave to the Lord whose it is and who will repay it.'[240] His ideas in *Jesus Christ the Same* are significant, since they disclose Bishop's earliest encounter with redefining his understanding of religious truth. Moreover, beneath the surface of his remarks there lies a glimpse of the pacifism and total denunciation of state interference in matters of conscience that would emerge a decade later. For the time being, however, in this and other pre-Restoration works, Bishop would continue to support the army's efforts and recognize the state as the guardian of religious liberty.

The movement's emphasis on organization, communication, and mutual support created the need for people with administrative experience. Bishop's ability to formulate and disseminate ideas in writing soon proved valuable to the Quakers. As he had done for the Commonwealth, he would now gather, assess, and transmit information to safeguard the security of Quakerism. He began this association, along with several Bristol shopkeepers, including Thomas Gouldney, Dennis Hollister, Capt. Edward Pyott, and Henry Roe, most likely the City Councilman who was dismissed in 1656.[241] This group worked closely to safeguard the movement from the hostility it met, and by 1656 they published *The Cry of Blood*, a standard account of the early history of Bristol Quakerism.

From this tract and from his other writings, we learn that liberty of conscience quickly became Bishop's major concern after he joined the Quakers, yet he still maintained his interest in securing the safety of the state. It is evident that he regarded the safety of one as guarantee for the well-being of the other. This outlook sharpened his disappointment since he felt the Protector, Council, and Parliament needlessly equivocated over religious reform. On a local level, he found, the chance for securing liberty of conscience was even more elusive. The Protectorate, he reminded Cromwell, owed its existence to people's desire for religious liberty. 'Had it not been for the hopes of liberty of conscience,' he reasoned, 'all the money in the nation would not have tempted men to fight upon such account as they engaged.'[242] Bishop became more disenchanted with the political situation as he saw the ministry and civil authorities withhold liberty of conscience from his brethren.

The *Cry of Blood* catalogues the earliest Quaker sufferings in Bristol. The ministers and magistrates regarded the disruption of church services as an unwelcome challenge and source of irritation. Responding that they had violated no laws except those that were aimed at prelates or Catholic priests, the Quakers sought, but rarely received, legal protection. Instead, they met the violent reaction of local toughs, who were often incited, and frequently left unchecked, by the authorities. Bishop pointed out that the Quakers were denied the legal protection guaranteed by the thirty-seventh article of the Instrument of Government. The Article stipulated that those who

> Profess faith in God by Jesus Christ (though differing in judgment from the doctrine, worship or discipline publicly held forth) shall not be restrained from, but shall be protected in, the profession of the faith and exercise of their religion; so as they abuse not this liberty to the civil injury of others and to the actual disturbance of the public peace on their parts: provided this liberty be not extended to popery or prelacy, nor to such as, under the profession of Christ, hold forth and practice licentiousness.[243]

Bishop found that in reality the Quakers became yet another religion that made its apperance in a city whose commercial interests made many merchants wary of innovation. In the 1656 *The Cry of Blood*, addressed to several city aldermen, Bishop and his collaborators traced the city's recent record of intolerance with reli-

64

gious innovation. During the past eighteen years, Bristol had witnessed 'Episcopacy persecuting Puritanism ... with reproaches, riots, imprisonments, and accusations of plotting against the kingdom.'[244] The tract discussed how the ambiguity towards conscience in the postwar religious settlement left Presbyterians and Independents making accusations of heresy and schism against each other and the radical sects in the city. However, the arrival of the Quakers with their outspoken criticisms and lack of deference proved so bothersome to these:

> Episcopals, Presbyterians, Independents, Baptists, Notionists, Ranters and rude rabble of ignorant and dissolute people, the priests and the rules aforesaid, [that they] reconciled, joined and folded together, as Herod, Pontious Pilate and the Jews in exercising the very same reproaches and persecutions wherein themselves suffered from each other ... against those who are called forth to witness Jesus now made manifest in them.[245]

Like other mid-seventeenth-century heterodox thinkers, Bishop believed the publication of truth was the instrument through which 'the kingdom of general darkness ... [would] be replaced by the republic of universal light.'[246] His work, he believed, would persuade the authorities to halt the religious persecution and violence that had characterized the introduction of Quakerism into Bristol. There is no evidence that Bishop himself was a victim of violence or was jailed during the 1650s, since his wife's influential relatives, or his own social standing in the community, may have saved him from such treatment. Nevertheless, in later years Bishop declined preferential treatment and a chance to return home while his less-influential brethren, with whom he had been at a meeting, remained in jail.[247] Other Bristol Quakers, however, became early 'sufferers' for their faith. Thus one of his earliest tasks in the organization of Bristol Quakerism was to construct a defense of the rights of those who were jailed.

He interpreted their disruption of church services as the fulfillment of a Christian's obligation to silence apostates and

65

enemies of truth. He supported his argument by comparing the heroism of early Christians, who aggressively confronted oppression, to the Quakers who disrupted church services.[248] Bishop also employed the theory of the inner light as part of his defense of those brethren who had been arrested for disrupting services. He explained that the indwelling Christ compelled them to stand as witnesses against those whose lies jeopardized the salvation of the faithful. Moreover, he reminded them that the disrupters invariably defied warning and contested their arrests because in actuality they had broken no law.[249] Hence in light of the unfair treatment they encountered, Bishop asked the authorities:

> How long will ye beat, tumult, imprison
> and cruelly intreat His witness, whom
> from amongst yourselves he hath raised
> up to testify against them into the paths
> of peace, and out of dear love to your soul
> press through all hardships and sufferings,
> and difficulties at your hands? Yea their
> lives are not dear to them for the finishing
> of their testimony and that your souls may
> be saved in this powerful day of the Lord
> Jesus.[250]

His notion of a 'witness's' obligation to challenge authority, whether it be a minister or a magistrate, was an early example of the distinction he would eventually make between spiritual and worldly constraints.[251]

Bishop chronicled a number of attacks made on the Quakers and sent an account of their sufferings to the city aldermen, who he hoped would see the injustice of religious persecution. His work reveals that the Quakers suffered the harsh conditions of seventeenth-century jails, healing each other's wounds in overcrowded dens of contagion. Some, like Temperance Hignall, he reported, 'were knocked down to the ground' by the 'rude multitude' and sustained injuries from which they never recovered.[252] His account of the severe beating and harsh conditions is consistent with extant private accounts and burial records. The Quaker sense of business included the careful keeping of birth, marriage, and burial records. The first recorded Quaker burial in Bristol was dated November 1655. The dead woman had been 'sorely beaten' after disrupting a service in Temple parish church. She subsequently died in Newgate prison as the result of the type of violence Bishop had been urging the authorities to restrain.[253]

Elizabeth Marshall, one of the first Quaker 'sufferers,' was assaulted by the angry parishoners at St. Nicholas. Marshall was thrown out into the street for disrupting preacher Ralph Farmer's service, and it was alderman and former mayor William Canne, Bishop's father-in-law, who 'commanded the people to lay hands on her.'[254] Mortimer has suggested: 'The persecution was based on Puritan jealousy of the influence of new teachers.'[255]

To respond to this violence, Bishop warned the authorities to closely examine the Presbyterian ministers who were provoking them against the Quakers. In his estimation they were continuing the work of the Catholic priests who had sought to frustrate Christian reform.[256]

Nonetheless, Bishop's effort to secure a peaceful recognition for the Quakers continued to be hampered by what he regarded as the lawlessness and violence that was corrupting the city. The situation that undoubtedly affected him most profoundly was the 1654 apprentice riots. The 'notorious and unparalleled tumults and insurrections' that began in December continued sporadically into January.[257]

The Cry of Blood provides a detailed account of the turmoil that began on December 18 as preachers Audland and Camm crossed over Bristol Bridge to attend a Quaker meeting in Somerset. A mob of apprentices confronted them with physical and verbal abuse. The actions of the apprentices quickly attracted a crowd. During a heated moment, they called out to hang Audland and Camm on the spot, and were about to drag them to Wine Street when calmer voices encouraged the rioters to bring the Quaker preachers before the mayor. Allegedly, Farmer was among the masters who provoked the attack.[258] The authorities arrested three rioters but did nothing to apprehend the ringleaders. Bishop condemned them for not enforcing the law or keeping the peace. He recalled that among them was Richard Newman, a chief constable, whose servant was among the rioters. Newman viewed the turmoil from his home but failed to intervene. Bishop remarked how the constable's servant was a 'chief rioter' and how 'those peaceable citizens who endeavored to pacify and stop the riot' were ignored.[259]

On the second day, when Audland and Camm again attempted to travel to Brislington, the riot resumed and was estimated at one time to involve over 1500 people. The mayor claimed to have an order from the Protector; however, Bishop noted that masters encouraged their apprentices to ignore any orders. They denied that the mayor had an order from Cromwell, and some publicly called out the name of Charles Stuart as King of England. The chief officers of the garrison, after petitioning the magistrates to restore order, tried to stop the riot themselves. They were concerned that it would soon be out of control, and they knew not 'what mischief such tumult might instigate ... or what design it might carry with it against the Commonwealth.'[260]

The anti-Quaker riot was viewed by all parties as a perfect occasion to stir the animosity that was harbored by those who rejected the Commonwealth's innovations. Historian Barry Reay has noted, 'the apprentices drew upon a natural reservoir of anti-military feeling that had intensified with the Bristol garrison's blatant support of the Quaker movement during the sect's early days in the city.'[261] Unfortunately, for the Quakers, the antimilitary mood in Bristol exacerbated the violence which they encountered. Finally two members of the City Council rode to Whitehall and presented a petition concerning the riots to the Protector. Consequently, he ordered Audland and Camm to leave Bristol.

Bishop was outraged at this decision. In *The Cry of Blood* he cited the Tudor law, 13 Hen 4.C.2., which required magistrates to: 'suppress a riot in their view, and to record the same ... [so] offenders may be punished.'[262] Moreover, he charged the liberties of 'freeborn Englishmen,' who had fought in the wars and had broken no law, had been violated.

It was evident that the authorities in Bristol were concerned about the spread of Quakerism and the sect's association with the military. The petition delivered by the city councilmen to the protector laid the blame for the riots on the presence of the military in the city. Thus, in addition to expelling Quaker preachers, the magistrates' interpretation of the riots prompted Cromwell to order Governor Scrope 'to move the garrison outside the city.'[263] After the riots, the Council and aldermen tightened precautions against strangers, creating situations that sometimes turned into imbroglios.

One such incident followed a Saturday evening Council meeting called by deputy mayor Richard Vickris, a wealthy city merchant, whose grandson and namesake would marry Bishop's daughter decades later. A fierce hater of Quakers, Vickris may have wanted 'to do something notable in the mayor's absence.' Falsely assuming that the leading Quakers, including Fox and Nayler, were congregating in the city, the Council ordered constables to a meeting on Corn Street, most probably at Bishop's home. Riots once again broke out as they searched the area for leading Quaker preachers, who were nowhere to be found. An order was issued in an attempt to keep Audland and Camm from returning to Bristol. Bishop was questioned and released by the authorities.[264]

The authorities were right to focus attention on Bishop. By the beginning of 1655 he was becoming a central figure in English Quaker affairs. The extent of Bishop's traveling with the Quakers is unclear, although we know that, in the early summer of 1655, he was with Fox at Reading, wearing his sword and using his military title.[265] He began receiving letters from co-religionists, including Pyott and Fox, and forwarded them to others for copying and circulation. He managed funds that were collected to finance the various needs of the growing movement. His home was used to hold meetings and to shelter traveling preachers. In all likelihood he met Margaret Fell during the summer 1655. She was probably in Bristol in July when Audland sent her regards in a letter to Burrough and Howgill.[266] By 1656, he was familiar enough with Fell to convey regards from his wife during the course of a routine exchange of letters and settling of accounts. Thus, entrusted with the sect's correspondence and contributions, and in touch with key members, Bishop was locally based but a central figure in the establishment of the Quaker community, in and beyond Bristol. The function he now performed for the Quakers resembled his previous service to the Commonwealth. Yet in the early months of 1655, while he was involved in the establishment of Quakerism, he was no less concerned for the safety of the Protectorate.

Since the autumn of 1653, a small, secret council of the king's supporters known as the Sealed Knot, had organized themselves for the purpose of a countrywide insurrection. They planned to attack strategic towns and garrisons. Nicholas Armorer, a key figure, worked in London, where plans were laid to center events in the north and west, particularly in the vicinity of the Welsh border. Naturally, royalist plans for insurrections were complicated by numerous problems, the least not being their own internal divisions. As was the case when Scot and Bishop headed the Committee for Examinations, intelligence agents under Thurloe worked increasingly to thwart their plans.

By February 1655, royalists and their supporters were in the vicinity of Bristol, reorganizing a 'western association.' In March, a group of them under the leadership of John Penruddock would stage an unsuccessful insurrection in Wiltshire. The plot, according to Woolrych, was 'only the small visible appearance of a vastly greater mass of conspiracy which remained below the surface.'[267] Bishop was alarmed by the growing number of royalists in the West Country. After Bishop sighted Edward Massey (the former Parliamentary soldier turned royalist supporter) and a young man believed to be the Duke of York, he mixed with royalists and picked up his pen to convey intelligence.[268]

In February 1655 some three or four hundred friends of the royalist Sir John Newton had gathered in the city to attend his mother's funeral. Local constables ordered to follow the strangers overheard boasting about royalist plans. Although the only problem they created was the accidental setting of a small fire, their presence worried Bishop. The intelligence he sent Thurloe discussed the local ambivalence toward the Commonwealth and presents a deep, perhaps exaggerated, concern for the hazards that the gathering royalists posed to the government.[269] On 17 February he wrote:

> We continue though at present quiet, yet every hour expecting a great storm to fall … you might perhaps think me too affectionate in what I've presented of danger here, but you know … this city and the parts about it and how easily in a few days an army of 20,000 horse and foot might be raised and furnished … without anything to make any considerable resistance.[270]

He signed off apologizing for his 'plainness' in reporting this trouble, but excused it as his 'affection to the Commonwealth.'[271]

Although Bishop called for the strengthening of the garrison, he was wary that the presence of 'arms, ammunition, men, money and other provisions of war' might serve the cause of the insurgents.[272] Nonetheless, Thurloe took Bishop's reports seriously enough and reinforced the garrison. Thus once again the military presence near Bristol was enlarged. To the chagrin of the city corporation that had struggled to have the garrison removed, a troublesome Quaker had instigated its return.

In February 1654, Maj. William Boteler arrived in Bristol. He had been sent to investigate the situation between the authorities and the radical sectaries. Additionally, he was told to evaluate the need to reinforce the garrison for the expected uprising. Upon inspection, he questioned the need to recruit more troops. The reports Bishop had been forwarding to Thurloe, he realized, were more alarming than his. He told Thurloe that he considered himself ill equipped for the task as he was 'a stranger in these parts and could not get such men as ... [he] might elsewhere; and would be loath to call any poor men from their callings and families unless there [was] a most absolute necessity and ... [I] might assure them pay.'[273]

He anticipated Thurloe's confusion over the differences in tone between his and Bishop's reports. On one occasion, he was careful to thank Thurloe for making him aware of the intelligence that called for greater vigilance against the royalists' designs. He even agreed that

> The continuance of the cavaliers' designs must needs continue my care and diligence to discover, prevent or break them ... I believe you will receive some complaint from GB [Bishop] and Mr. Hollister as soon as they understand what representation I have made of the affairs here.[274]

Caught in the middle of the bickering between the Bristol authorities on one side, and the army and the radicals on the other, he commented that it was impossible for him to 'escape without censures on one side, though my conscience tells me, I deserve them on neither.'[275] Upon his arrival in Bristol he attempted to adjudicate the situation by listening to the various complaints of the involved parties. He heard Bishop, Hollister, and their friends complain that the magistrates were withholding their liberties and disregarding the law. He spoke to the magistrates and concluded that malice did not motivate their actions. In a final attempt to gain a clear sense of their respective grievances, Boteler called a meeting and invited all disaffected parties. Bishop and Hollister, who apparently sensed the likemindedness between Boteler and the magistrates, declined to attend, claiming they were 'indisposed to the motion.' Boteler's account of the meeting suggests there was a deep intolerance for Quakers in the otherwise religiously tolerant major.[276]

He reported that the accusation of religious intolerance against the mayor and aldermen was unfounded. He considered their opponents' complaints to be tedious, and was annoyed with his fellow officers' corroboration of them. Having discovered no apparent royalist plot, and disgusted by the army's protection of the sectarians, he cautioned Thurloe against the unnecessary expense and danger of keeping the town castle as a fort. Instead he recommended that should the government decide to keep the garrison, they find 'some other employment' for Captains Beale and Watson. Referring to what he surely perceived as the officers' complicity in the Quaker menace, he denounced their 'dishonor of religion, your Highness, the army, and I must needs say, that it hath been only the goodness of God that such carriages have not begotten more than animosities from his people [the magistrates].'[277] He then turned directly to the Quakers, whose 'rage and railing' against both ministers and magistrates disturbed the peace of public places.[278] The report of his findings aroused additional suspicions about the Quakers, and henceforth toleration became increasingly elusive in Bristol.

Calling Bishop 'half a Quaker,' Boteler reminded Thurloe of this past criticisms of the 'present government.' He viewed Bishop's religious conversion as an occasion 'to have a party to make a little opposition … [against] the town.'[279] Regarding him with the utmost suspicion, he dismissed the 'probability' of the intelligence Bishop conveyed. Boteler's suspicion of Bishop becomes clearest when read in the context of the entire report to Thurloe. Immediately following his comment concerning Bishop, Boteler turned to a separate yet related issue: the apprehension and arrest of John Wildman.[280]

72

In September 1654, the republican John Wildman was among the MPs who were denied entrance to the House after they refused to agree in writing that they would not attempt to alter the government. Subsequently, Wildman drafted a petition that three army colonels presented to Cromwell in which they protested the exclusion of the nonsigning members and the April 1653 dissolution of the Rump. Members of the army who had denounced the establishment of the Protectorate and the exclusion of MPs thought the Protector was exercising arbitrary powers that went beyond those which had been wielded by the late king.[281] The replacement of legal, hereditary kingship with Cromwell's *de facto* leadership provoked comparisons with Machiavellian politics. Cromwell's conduct and decisions in the complex political situation of the Interregnum were often strongly criticized by his own partisans as well as by his opponents.[282]

Naturally, intelligence agents had monitored the petitioners' meetings. Bishop, they found, was among the disenchanted republicans who had taken an interest in the affair. Thurloe learned that he had brought a draft of the petition to Bradshaw for inspection. The petitioners wanted:

> A full and free Parliament ... [to] consider ... those fundamental rights and freedoms of the Commonwealth that are the first subject of this great contest, which God hath decided on our side, according as the same have been proposed to the Parliament by the Grand Council of the Army in the Agreement of the People.[283]

In early 1655, Wildman was pursued by the authorities, and his associates in the affair lost their commissions.[284] Hence the fact that Boteler's negative assessment of Bishop's character was reported along with the apprehension of Wildman suggests that, like other radicals who had criticized the policies of the Protector and his advisors, Bishop was no longer trusted by the authorities.

Less than one month after Boteler's reluctance to request additional men and supplies for defense of the West Country, the royalists under Penruddock's leadership made their move. In the early hours of March 12, a group of some one hundred and eighty insurgents rode into Salisbury and positioned guards in strategic points in the city. Proclaiming that Charles Stuart was king, they awoke and manhandled two assize judges and burned their commissions. Next they set loose prisoners whose gratitude they sought to exchange for support. With their motley recruits, and a sheriff held as hostage, they rode out of town. Among their many misfortunes was their failure to attract the support of powerful local figures whose influence would have strengthened their chances of toppling the Protectorate. Missing even the chance to escape, they were caught by the expectant troops who rode out from various counties. In three days' time, Cromwell's troops ended a rising that had taken months of planning.[285]

Much of the information Bishop sent to Thurloe was gathered from travelers who passed through the vicinity of the uprising. On March 14, he speculated on the areas in the west where the pockets of royalist support were greatest. He observed that there was a wide disparity among the numbers of reported insurgents. Yet regarding the accuracy and integrity of his previous communication, he remarked: 'We have lately seen an unexpected issue on our representation of danger, which were no dreams or fancies. We know what we wrote, though the hand hath been turned against us.'[286]

The intelligence Bishop reported in connection with Penruddock's Rising was convincing enough to effect the reinforcement of the city garrison. But despite the validity of his reports, and seemingly earnest intentions, the arrival of soldiers brought Bishop the animosity of his neighbors, who were becoming increasingly irritated with both the army and the Quakers. Only a few days after the frightening royalist attack, Thurloe received word of the increased discontent caused by the 'superadded officers' who accompanied the reinforcements. The soldiers angered the authorities in Bristol by protecting strangers in the city, particularly itinerant preachers and their followers who now came and went from the city with alarming frequency. The soldiers were viewed as opportunists who readily used force, and, according to Farmer, the garrison's officers mixed with the 'professed enemies of the present authority [namely] that viper Bishop and that gang [of Quakers].'[287]

CHAPTER FIVE

'Looking After a Kingdom That Cannot Be Shaken': The Early Quakerism of George Bishop

IN FEBRUARY 1655 Bishop wrote to Thurloe regarding how those who professed loyalty to the present government were aiding royalist insurgents. He expressed concern for the Protectorate's safety, stressing 'the [pro]portion of that interest [the royalist supports] and all that join to it.'[288] Yet by this date Bishop's spiritual well-being had become his primary concern. Adding that political 'discouragements and temptations ... [had] not been a few or trivial,' he told Thurloe that he was now 'looking after a kingdom that cannot be shaken and [was] studying peace with truth.'[289] Framing his inward journey in millinarian imagery, Bishop explained that, upon his arrival, Christ would be enthroned in the hearts and minds of those like himself who pursued righteousness and denounced hypocrisy. In this kingdom there would be none of the inequity and corruption that had disturbed him since the late 1640s. Bishop's letter rendered him suspect at Whitehall, and in the following months both Thurloe and Cromwell repeatedly ordered him to return state papers.

On 22 May Thurloe demanded that Bishop return papers that had formerly belonged to the Archbishop of Canterbury. Bishop replied that the papers were not in his possession and suggested that Scot might have them. Obviously concerned over the distrust that was implicit in the requests for official papers that Cromwell and his secretary had been making, Bishop promised Thurloe he would surrender papers he had brought to Bristol with him, 'which are most of them of little use.'[290]   He urged Thurloe to 'cause that warrant [to deliver the papers] to be withdrawn, this being the truth of the matter.'[291]   Clearly, as his new ties with Quakers were formed, Bishop's old ties with the Protectorate were severed.

Bishop's association with Quakerism came at a time when the movement, which may have gathered as many as 60,000 followers by 1660, was experiencing rapid growth.[292] Distrusted by the authorities, on 14 June 1654, the Quakers made their first appearance in the proceedings of the Council of State when a committee was appointed to investigate how 'the meetings of Quakers, which were becoming so numerous might best be suppressed.'[293]

Yet it was the Quakers' comportment, not their numbers, that was most alarming to their detractors.   They frequently employed nonverbal symbolic gestures in place of words to express their search for simplistic living and spiritual truth.[294]   Unlike Catholic, Anglican, or Presbyterian services that were characterized by sermons or biblical explication, the Quakers worshipped in silence. Inasmuch as their testimonies were the manifestations of the internal Christ, they did not regard the words they delivered to be their own. Thus, in Quakerism speaking and literalness were replaced by what one scholar described as 'metaphorical sign performances.'[295]

These metaphorical expressions sometimes included the destruction of physical objects. For instance, a Quaker might tear apart his hat rather than doff it to show that magistrates should be more concerned with uncovering injustice than with receiving deference.[296] Others went naked as a sign to protest what they saw as the bare truth of some form of corruption. At other times, they used their trembling bodies to demonstrate that they were filled with 'the movings of the Lord.' They made prophecies and delivered warnings about events they believed would incur God's anger.[297] For instance, Bishop said that 'Through the mouth of the Lord of hosts' he had learned that God would punish Cromwell if he continued 'to hearken and to follow and to be guided by' the spirit that blinded rulers and turned them against liberty of conscience.[298]

In the seventeenth century, spirits, good and bad, were thought to inhabit the universe. Cunning men and women were still consulted by their superstitious neighbors to break spells or to foretell the future. During this time when life was filled with the numerous hardships that accompany war, plague, and scarcity, people were quick to blame their misfortunes on the malice of a person who had cast an evil eye or animated the devil's agents. Those who were regarded as witches or victims of satanic possession were frequently people who exhibited eccentric behavior or had magnetic personalities. More often than not they were women.[299] Thus it is not surprising that Quaker preachers were accused of casting spells on their converts and serving them liquids from odd bottles.[300] One contemporary account recalled how 'a man of good parts,' one who was given to 'novelties,' went 'to hear these people called Quakers [and] was presently bewitched by them, that he ran up and down the town in a confused manner crying out very blasphemously 'I am the way, the truth and the life' and thus continued ... sometimes running naked about the streets ... being as he said so commanded to do so by a voice within him ... the voice of the devil.'[301] In *Religion and the Decline of Magic*, historian Keith Thomas has noted that the Quakers' bodily convulsions, fasting, and religious prophecies subjected many of them to accusations of sorcery, which sometimes resulted in the accused being brought to trial.[302]

Cromwell's response to the Quakers and other radical sects was ambiguous. On the one hand, he was repelled by what he considered fanatical behavior, yet he understood the protection of religious liberty as his godly obligation. In an attempt to mitigate the suffering of jailed Quakers, Bishop reproached Cromwell and reminded him how he had formerly 'plead[ed] the cause of the Lord's oppressed and of His kingdom in the consciences of men ... [and saw it] as near at hand and often ... [declared that it was] the design and end of the Lord in the wars.'[303] Liberty of conscience was further jeopardized when Cromwell's first Protectorate Parliament neglected to define the limits of toleration or the nature of damnable heresy. Thus is 1654 and early 1655 the unclear policy of religious liberty enabled the justices in Bristol and other counties to detain or imprison the Quakers and other sects.[304] Cromwell's proclamation of 15 February 1655 gave official approval to the intolerance of the local officials, explaining that the Quakers and Ranters who disturbed Christian services and preachers 'dispensing the word' were disturbing the peace. Since these distrubances were 'contrary to the just freedom and liberties of the people,' Cromwell publicly declared his disapproval of 'such practices' and required offending parties to discontinue them. It stipulated that if these Quakers and Ranters should 'presume to offend as aforesaid, we shall esteem them disturbers of the civil peace, and shall expect and do require all officers and ministers of justice to proceed against them accordingly.'[305]

In Bristol Bishop chided the authorities, who disregarded the civil rights of the Quakers they arrested. He was angered that it had become common practice to arrest them without producing the required warrants; and they routinely were sent to jail without being told what law they had broken. The authorities turned a deaf ear to the Quaker pleadings for justice, and, in one instance, the exasperated mayor responded to a plea for a *mittimus* by stating that his word served as one.[306] Bishop argued that, because they were denied their just liberties, many of those who had risked their lives in the Parliamentary army were now being treated as enemies of the republic. In *The Cry of Blood*, he condemned the magistrates for the October 1655 arrest of John Smith, who had served in the Parliamentary army. Smith was brought before the mayor of Bristol for disturbing a religious service, and was denied a *mittimus*. As he was being led away, he turned to his accusers and condemned their refusal to identify his crime as a breach of his civil rights. Bishop found it a bitter irony that Whitehall had abandoned Parliamentary soldiers who suffered injustice at the hands of royalist sympathizers. He described how the distraught Smith called out upon his arrest that 'he did not venture his life and lose his blood to set up his enemies to rule over him.'[307]

In early 1654 Bishop was at work trying to relieve the suffering of the growing number of Quakers who were jailed for disrupting services, conducting meetings, or refusing to pay tithes. He disbursed money to them for their court and jail fees and coordinated the charitable efforts of brethren who contributed their time and money to mitigate their suffering. Most importantly, he tried to win the support of justices who might be sympathetic to what he saw as a violation of their religious liberties.[308]

In January 1656, Fox, Pyott, and Thomas Salt, a London Quaker, disregarded a local ban in Cornwall and delivered 'a paper for the directing ... [of] minds to the way of salvation and the stirring of them up to prize their time and the day of their visitation.'[309]

While being questioned by local authorities, the Quakers angered them by refusing to remove their hats and by addressing their superiors with the familiar 'thou.' Fox and his group were jailed for disturbing the peace in Doomsdale dungeon at Launceton, where they remained for eight months. On their way to Launceton to visit Fox, Nayler and some companions stopped at Exeter and were arrested on vague charges of vagabondage.[310] Thus with the two leading Quaker preachers in jail, Bishop's efforts to win the support of sympathetic justices was of grave importance to the future of the movement.[311]

Bishop sent the prisoners funds, and they, in turn, sent him news of their plight to use as documentation in the appeal to the authorities. The conditions at Doomsdale were notoriously bad. Usually reserved for accused witches and murderers, the place had not been cleaned out for years. Pyott told Bishop that 'the stink of the felon's room underneath comes up so strong, [and the boards] be so open, and they are so nasty in the lower room, as that I think the stink is stronger above than below.'[312]

In May, Bishop sent the prisoners 10 pounds to cover expenses that would ease their suffering. The justices, who were somewhat more sympathetic to the Quakers than the jailers, eventually accepted Quaker money to open the door and permit the prisoners' brethren to clean out their cell and purchase their food in town. Pyott declined the money Bishop sent, as he was able to fund his own expenses from his business, which in his absence was kept by his wife and by his fellow Quaker, Thomas Speed.[313]

Bishop also disbursed funds to Nayler and the others at Exeter jail. They too had been sending him reports of their continued work in the service of truth and their prison experiences for publication. At Exeter, where conditions were somewhat better than at Doomsdale, Quakers reported that for ten shillings a week they had 'a room to be private in, where we meet three days in a week and any have liberty to come to us … [as] they do bar us not from speaking.'[314]

In August 1656, while Bishop coordinated the disbursal of funds to traveling and imprisoned preachers, he was also at work devising a plan in which 'London friends and Bristol friends might go equal in their disbursements for prisoners at Exeter.'[315] Occasionally, a Quaker's need was questioned by Bishop and the others who controlled the movement's finances. Apparently there were those who sought to abuse this goodwill and were less than sincere in their intentions.[316]

From the correspondence between Bishop and Edward Pyott, his neighbor and collaborator on *The Cry of Blood*, we learn of the lead Bishop took in the writing, editing, and printing of the major Quaker tract, *The West Answering to the North*. Pyott and Fox sent Bishop various detailed letters and documents, along with careful instructions for preparation of the tract's publication. Fox was aware that this was a dangerous time for him to publicize his prison experiences. Yet he believed that they contained vital information for Quakers throughout England, Ireland, Scotland, and overseas. Fox's influence was, of course, a source of annoyance to the government. Thus in preparing *The West Answering to the North* for publication, Bishop followed a schedule that was sensitive to the calendar of the justices. The imprisoned Quakers, and perhaps the future of the movement, sorely needed the understanding and good will of the justices in the counties. Displaying political acumen, he published *The West Answering to the North* after the assize court had passed through Launceton.[317]

Bishop arranged the tract as an anthology of violations against the jailed Quakers' liberties. Internal travel, even for those who held passes from Cromwell, was becoming increasingly difficult. The abuse of this 'birth right,' he explained, demonstrated to the Quakers that the magistrates held in contempt the laws that so many had died defending. Like numerous JPs who had committed Quakers to various English jails, Peter Ceely confined Fox and his companions to Launceton 'without any just ground, color or pretense in law, justice or equity.'[318]

Bishop clearly illustrated that, despite Cromwell's 12 September 1654 declaration to Parliament that liberty of conscience was one of the four fundamentals of his government, 'which he had set up as the issue of the late wars and blood,' in actuality local magistrates like Ceely were misusing their power to 'obstruct' religious liberty. Able to bypass the protector's promises and article thirty-seven of the Instrument of Government, local magistrates he explained, were also foolishly ignoring the prophecies that foretold the punishment destined for those who opposed the efforts of the godly.[319]

In the tract Bishop also included a copy of a letter that had been sent to John Glynn, the Chief Justice of England. The letter explained how Glynn's assize court had violated the rights that Fox, Pyott, and Salt possessed as freeborn Englishmen. It appears that, when the court met at Launceton, standard procedures had been ignored and the prisoners' books had been confiscated. The letter explained that the Quakers' refusal to remove their hats was not done out of contempt for the court's authority, but as a sign of respect to God. Their right to follow their conscience in this matter had been sealed with the blood of those who had fought in the late wars. Cromwell himself, Glynn was reminded, had called liberty of conscience a 'natural right.' However, the chief justice was told that both rights and laws were being 'adulterated by lawyers, as the Scriptures were mangled by the priests.'[320]

In July 1656, while Fox, Pyott, and Nayler were still in jail, Bishop wrote an appeal to Cromwell. On behalf of the imprisoned Quakers, he expressed his anger that the fight for liberty of conscience had received such poor recompense. He reminded Cromwell that 'when the wars ended for liberty of conscience, [we] had little reason to expect such dealing as we now receive from such a generation who by the sword fought … for our conscience.'[321]

Referring to numerous jailed Quakers, he boldly included Cromwell as an accomplice to their unjust suffering.

> The ears will tingle of all that hear all that hath been inflicted herein by judges, officers, the rude multitude, jailors, thievers and murders … Some [Quakers] have had pistols presented to their mouths by the troopers, heaved out of their meetings, and with blasphemous damnings have the troopers sworn that there they should die if they did not deny their religion … and of many of these things thou hast not been ignorant.[322]

In the July 1656 letter Bishop condemned Cromwell for ignoring the reports he received of Quaker persecution. Referring to the those who had authored appeals or traveled to London and delivered their 'messages,' Bishop told him, 'They have laid many of these things before thee … some in writing, others by verbal declaration … But has thou heard?'[323] Seemingly unconcerned with the political pressures the Protector confronted at Whitehall, as well as in the counties, Bishop chided Cromwell for not guaranteeing full liberty of conscience. In Bishop's view Cromwell's failure to defend the liberty of the faithful proved his contempt for laws of the land. He reminded him that he too had 'suffered and groaned' under the monarchy until the judgment of God had brought an end to the king and the bishops. Now it was a sad irony that God's very instrument of justice had turned on his friends, an act which rendered Cromwell more culpable than Charles Stuart.

> Nor were they [the Puritans and the late king] ever one in principle, spirit and action, especially in such a one and in such action as thou and we have been ... Yet we do (thus) suffer at thine hands whom we have loved above any man ... and thy lot and portion we have chosen to stand or fail, as it should be unto thee. And so have we stood by thee against all thine opposers, whether in field or in council. Thine enemies we have accounted and made our own.[324]

With the Quakers under constant threat of arrest, and with important figures like Fox and Nayler in jail, Bishop assumed a leading role in Quaker organization. In addition to the controlling of funds and the passing on of letters to Fell for copying and circulation, he coordinated the efforts of Quakers in London who were charged with eliciting the support of sympathetic justices and ministers.[325] Through a lengthy account that Bishop wrote to Margaret Fell, he apprised Judge Fell of the recent arrest, trials, and imprisonments. He also conveyed his sense that liberty of conscience was becoming more elusive as 'authors' everywhere struck their 'swords' against 'the seed which is come to reign forever and ever.'[326] Bishop found that his own travel on behalf of the movement would have to be postponed because of the worsening situation. He expressed his regret to Margaret Fell that he could not travel north to visit with their brethren since 'friends are clapped up daily which makes my service the greater, and I have here as much as I can turn to.'[327] In September 1656 he told Fell that his role in the Quaker community had settled him more firmly into the 'unshakeable kingdom,' and had enabled him to sustain worldly disappointment.[328]

When he first became associated with the Quakers, Bishop had expressed his devotion in what his contemporaries described as an 'exalted' manner. Braithwaite has asserted that 'Elizabeth Morgan of Chester, who bred dissension in Bristol meeting in 1655 by her unwise conduct and exalted spirit ... led George Bishop astray for a time'.[329] It is not surprising that the Quakers blamed Morgan, who they believed put 'black strength about ... [the arms of] those she bewitched' for Bishop's deviance.[330] In and outside of the Quaker movement female prophets like Morgan were frequently feared as witches or despised for what was regarded as hysterical or delusional behavior.[331] Thus it was not unusual that Bishop's demeanor was attributed to the influence of a woman who 'went on with much boldness.'[332]

Nonetheless Bishop was soon drawn to the quiet, temperate Quakerism that was preached by Fox and Burrough. In his search for truth he continued to testify against a ministry paid by tithes, and he maintained that, like 'the prophets, and Christ Jesus and the apostles and holy men of God did all ages before the altar in the temple and synagogues,' the Quakers were obliged to disturb any hypocrisy that was preached in God's name.[333]

Yet despite his recognition of the Christian obligation to denounce false teaching, Bishop was wary of what he regarded as the 'darkness,' 'filth,' and 'imaginations' of some Quakers. These brethren refused to remove their hats during prayer and broke other Quaker conventions.[334] Often, while their brethren delivered their divine inspirations of the inner light, these groups of outspoken Quakers would ridicule them.[335]

According to Bishop, James Nayler and a group of enthusiastic followers, many of whom were women, were among the Quakers who had gone 'out of truth in which light we believe and which light we follow after.'[336] Several of Nayler's followers, in particular Martha Calvert Simmonds, accompanied Nayler on his travels and were behaving like the adoring women of Jerusalem who had followed Christ. They had transcended metaphor and were venerating Nayler as if he were the embodiment of the second coming. Bishop condemned Nayler's failure to temper their adoration and regarded the group's behavior as an unhealthy blend of delusion and idolatry.[337]

Bishop's service to the imprisoned Quakers and his work on *The West Answering to the North* made him aware of the consequences that such behavior might provoke. In a tone that was reminiscent of his sentiments for the safety of the fragile Commonwealth, he referred to the young movement as the 'tender plants of the Lord.'[338] He recognized that preaching and prophesizing in a conspicuous or extravagant way could result in violence or imprisonment. Moreover, it increased the chance that Parliament would restrict rather than broaden the limits of toleration.

During the summer of 1656, Bishop met with Fox at Reading, where they discussed their mutual concern over Nayler and his companions. Although the Quakers did not have an established church structure for almost two decades, and there was no codified guide to discipline until 1738, it has been noted that 'evidences of discipline being set up to be guided by overseers and traveling ministers appear as early as 1652 and 1656.'[339] In an effort to protect themselves from their detractors, we are reminded, the Quakers took care of 'the fine detail of administration' and, likewise, the careful auditing of personal conduct.[340] In the 1650s leading Quakers like Bishop occasionally reproved their brethren concerning their conduct or method of devotion. Thus, like the elders of later decades who used their discernment to admonish, rebuke, or reprove those who had gone out of truth, Bishop and Fox chided Nayler for not discouraging the adulation of his followers. Fox warned Nayler that his 'willfulness and stubbornness' would satisfy his worldly vanity at the expense of truth.[341]

Bishop's concern for the damage that Nayler could do to the safety of the movement with its emphasis on the preservation of truth was sharpened by his recognition of Nayler's effectiveness as a preacher and writer. Even after his denunciation of Nayler he would remark:

> What mouth was there (then) opened against him [Nayler] that he did not condemn? What pen replied again when he had answered? ... And what he (then) wrote and what he ... spoke and ministered of the eternal life shall abide forever and shall have an eternal witness in that God in every man's conscience.'[342]

In July, shortly before Nayler was arrested at Exeter, Quakers who had been concerned about his conduct and that of his companions 'plucked' him from Simmonds' house and took him to Bristol.[343] There, according to Bishop, 'the darkness getting about him quick and sudden ... was seen by friends there [Bristol] how it had encompassed him. And that spirit ... was then denied by them.'[344] Before long, Simmonds followed him. Bishop and his brethren were determined to separate Nayler from Simmonds and removed him to another location in the city. Historian Phyllis Mack has noted that the Quakers' condemnation of the influence Simmonds had on Nayler was another example of what they regarded as 'the ranting spirit' of women. Simmonds, however, saw her hold on Nayler in a positive way and asserted that the power of Christ had risen in her spirit and gave the words 'which pierced and struck him down from that day.'[345] Bishop recalled how a 'darkness' which emanted from Simmonds had corrupted Nayler and that only after the Quakers had separated them did Nayler recover 'some sensibleness' and recapture 'the spirit which led out from God.'[346]

While writing *The West Answering to The North* and appealing to the assize justices to release the imprisoned Quakers, Bishop was concerned that Nayler and his followers might be drawing attention to themselves at Exeter. In August 1656 he questioned Nicholas Gannicliff, a West Country Quaker who was also detained at Exeter, about Nayler. Gannicliff praised Nayler and told Bishop that after a nineteen day fast, 'truly he [Nayler] is in a fine condition, an innocent lamb he is as I have seen.'[347] In what appears to be an attempt to allay Bishop's apprehension, he added 'I think he is not as many thought.'[348] Bishop was fearful that the behavior of Simmonds and some others who had traveled to Exeter would alienate the magistrates, and, of course, this would be detrimental to those in jail. In a second letter from Gannicliff, Bishop learned that Nayler's followers were 'seldom from him, but here abide as if they were prisoners ... He is not the better for it.'[349] Gannicliff withheld a direct answer, however, to Bishop's question concerning Nayler's behavior. Instead he wrote: 'As in answer to thy request about James Nayler, how it is with him, I shall say little. It is not my practice to write of things of that nature.'[350]

On October 24, newly released from Exeter jail, Nayler rode into Bristol on a horse, with followers, including Simmonds, Dorcas

Erbury, and Hannah Stranger, walking knee-deep in mud, laying their garments before him and chanting: 'Holy, holy, holy, Hosannah.'[351] After Nayler was arrested by the Bristol authorities he explained that his entry—a sign in honor of Christ—had been inspired by his internal spirit.[352]

News of the incident spread quickly. Bishop was angry because his efforts to quiet their 'exalted manner' had been ignored by the 'darkened' spirit of Nayler and by 'that woman and her company.'[353] Bishop worried that the chance of winning the support of magistrates who might befriend the Quakers had been severely damaged. With the organization and consolidation of the movement in jeopardy, Bishop became involved in a protracted defense of Quaker principles. Hoping 'to clear the innocent,' he formulated a denunciation of Nayler's actions and forwarded it to Margaret Fell. Bishop made it clear that, with regard to the practices of Nayler and his companions, 'we have not fellowship but the contrary.'[354]

His description has become a standard account of the episode. Its rich details reveal Bishop's outrage that, despite the warnings Nayler had received, he had gone ahead and jeopardized the Quakers' safety.

> The powers of darkness ... is come upon these parts. For you may understand that on the sixth day of the last week between the second and third hour in the afternoon, J. N. and his company (being released at Exeter) came into this town with full purpose and resolution to set up their image and to break the truth in pieces ... the mystery of iniquity which worked was brought forth ... [that] we sought formerly to have covered and judged down ... now was brought before the sun and which the world desired and the enemy sought after.[355]

There is no mistaking Bishop's intention of using the letter as a statement of the official Quaker position so that Fell and other leading Quakers might circulate it among their brethren. 'None go to visit them (as I can hear of) and whichever is of God is raised and stirred up against this work of darkness.'[356] His account is reminiscent of his activities at Whitehall, when he gathered intelligence and evaluated the movements of those who threatened the safety of the godly commonwealth.

> As to their other questions, they obtained nothing of advantage from him, for he was subtle, few in words and low ... I have endeavored to get copies [of Nayler's examination] ... that [we] ... might have the certainty ... If I can procure, it's like[ly] I may send copies [to] you ... of this thing as it proceeds ... To J.A. [John Audland] I have wrote particularly who it is like[ly] may inform thee.[357]

As Bishop and his fellow organizers had anticipated, their enemies were quick to use Nayler's example to launch an attack on the Quakers. Regarding the episode, one scholar has commented 'The moves against Nayler were clearly a prelude to a broader attack on the Quakers against whom petitions and pamphlets were produced with notable efficiency and shrewd timing.'[358] Among the numerous tracts that began to appear in late 1656 was *The Devil Turned Quaker*. It claimed that Nayler's ride was the logical outcome of heretical principles and practices. It argued that the Quakers distanced themselves from God's salvation when they replaced the authority of Scripture with their belief in the divinity of the inner light. That error, it explained, had alienated the Quakers from 'Our savior Jesus Christ, who is God ... impiously and blasphemously saying, God is in them and the Light within them is God.'[359]

In addition to bringing about their own spiritual destruction, the tract maintained that the Quakers posed a threat to society. Their 'odious and beast-like manner,' had time and again shown its scorn for authority. 'They are loose and lascivious in their lives and conversation, despising both ministry and magistracy.'[360] Their nonconformity was abhorred by their enemies because their lack of convention was often considered as a sign of witchcraft or sorcery. A query posed in *The Devil Turned Quaker* regarding the spell-like appearance of Quaker converts was based on the contemporary belief in the existence of supernatural forces.

The Quakers themselves believed they could employ magic against those who opposed them.[361] Hence, given the imagery that was created by Nayler and his followers, and the contemporary belief in magic, it is understandable that the author of *The Devil Turned Quaker* would ask: 'What witchery or sorcery is there among many of them, so that those that have but come to see them have been bewitched.'[362] According to Leviticus, the author maintained, this Quaker 'ringleader' should be stoned to death.

The anti-Nayler pamphlets, and the Bristol magistrates' decision to refer the matter to Parliament, soon confirmed Bishop's assertion that Nayler's actions would 'bruise and hand down and beguile and devour the tender plants of the Lord.'[363] The referral to Parliament, which the authorities in Bristol attributed to their 'confusion, shock and incompetence,' drew national attention to the Quakers.[364] Undoubtedly to Bishop's regret, the magistrates complained of the 'horrid and open blasphemies expressly avowed and owned' by Nayler and his followers.[365] The authorities noted how the support of the army and the absence of a law to restrain the Quakers had brought about their increase. The Quakers had been 'strengthened and encouraged' in Bristol since England was 'destitute of a law to punish and restrain them.' Consequently, the magistrates stated their 'unbridled liberties' threatened the Christian principles upon which the government was secured.[366] The Bristol magistrates' petition to Parliament was surely typical of anti-Quaker sentiment and the desire to curb liberty of conscience that existed in the provinces. It was also the negative publicity for the movement that Bishop had sought to avert. The petitioners admonished the House for its failure to meet a fundamental obligation and implored them to

> now take up the reins of government into
> your hands, which have too long lain loose
> in this particular and to curb the insolen-
> cies of all ungodly persons, who in this or
> any other way do or may eclipse the glory
> of our Christian profession.[367]

On 31 October Parliament ordered that a committee investigate 'the great misdemeanors and blasphemies of James Nayler and others at Bristol and elsewhere and make subsequent report on how their actions violated laws and ordinances made against blasphemy.'[368]

For several weeks, employing a variety of Biblical, moral, and legal precedents, the second Protectorate Parliament debated whether or not Nayler was guilty of 'horrid blasphemy.' There were some members in this Parliament who had not sat since Pride's 1648 purge, and together with the Presbyterians in the City of London, they wanted to narrow religious tolerance and to reverse what they regarded as 'the sectarian excess[es] and military rule' of the intervening years.[369] The first Protectorate Parliament had also sought to narrow the religious liberty that was outlined in articles thirty-seven and thirty-eight of the Instrument of Government.

Extending toleration, and granting the liberty that permitted people to follow their consciences, were despised ideas to many of Bishop's contemporaries. Even toleration, which the historian W.K. Jordan has reminded us is the more conservative of the two liberties, since it makes an allowance without giving official recognition to one's beliefs, was commonly seen as a force of the antichrist that threatened the sanctity of both church and state.[370] In October 1654, when the religious articles in the Instrument were about to be reviewed, the London Presbyterians made it a point to list all the heresies that existed in England.[371] The most feared of the heresies was Socinianism with its antitrinitarian doctrine that challenged the divinity of the historical Christ and the Holy Ghost.[372] Nayler's ride into Bristol was to many a display of the Quakers' antitrinitarianism. Hence, as Bishop surely realized, the episode provided Parliament with a pretext for arguing how heresy was occasioned by religious liberty.

Among Nayler's staunchest critics in the Parliamentary proceedings were Robert Aldworth, the Bristol MP to whom Bishop had lost the 1654 election; and Philip Skippon, the military commander whom Bishop praised in his 1645 Naseby tract. A strong opponent of the Quakers, Skippon considered them part of a group of radical extremists who sought to subvert law and order. He declared that the Instrument of Government had given too much liberty to 'these Quakers, Ranters, Levellers, Socinians and all sorts,' and now the House was under a moral and legal obligation to reverse this dangerous situation. He wrote

I heard the supreme magistrate [Cromwell] say, It was never his intention to indulge such things, yet we see the issue of the liberty of conscience. It sits hard upon my conscience, and I choose rather to venture my discretion than betray conscience by my silence. If this be liberty, God deliver me from such liberty. It is to evil, not to good, that this liberty extends.[373]

Parliament had accepted the Bristol magistrates' petition, and Nayler was currently before them presenting his testimony. Bishop wanted to defend the Quaker movement and the securing of liberty of conscience, so he assumed the responsibility of petitioning the House on their behalf. Alarmed by the Bristol magistrates' call for anti-Quaker legislation, and possibly news from Whitelocke, Desborough or other acquaintances in the House, Bishop wrote to Parliament on 8 December. In defense of 'truth, equity and justice,' he proposed that his letter be read during the proceedings. Although he maintained his disapproval of Nayler's actions, he warned Parliament 'to take heed [of] condemning the accused unheard [the Quakers, not Nayler and his group] or ... of entertain[ing] prejudice against a suffering people who fear before the Lord, and have always been faithful to the Commonwealth.[374] Bishop later commented

the rise and end of my writing ... was not in the behalf of J.N. and those with him, but in our own, the people called Quakers in Bristol and the truth we witnessed.[375]

Aware that their detractors would assert that 'the false and feigned' actions of Nayler was sufficient testimony of the Quakers' hypocritical understanding of truth, Bishop hoped to persuade them to demonstrate clemency.

On 17 December 1656, Nayler was called to the bar after what had become a curiously long and heated debate. Found guilty of blasphemy, and escaping the penalty of death by only 14 votes, he was sentenced to life imprisonment. This part of his sentence would be preceded by severe and humiliating punishment in both London and Bristol.[376] On 25 December, Cromwell expressed his concern that Parliament might have exceeded their authority in the Nayler case. Although he agreed that 'the least countenance [should not be given] to persons of such opinions and practices,' he questioned Parliament's neglect to seek his counsel in the affair. He wrote

> We being entrusted in the present govern-
> ment on behalf of the people of these
> nations, not knowing how far such
> proceedings (wholly without us) may
> extend ... do desire that the House will let
> us know on what grounds and reasons
> whereupon they have proceeded.[377]

Parliament, however, remained silent concerning their possible abuse of authority, and the Protector pursued the matter no further.

As it turned out, the religious legislation that followed the trial was more conservative, and Bishop found that the chance of securing a religious settlement that would satisfy the Quakers and other sectaries was more remote. Current interpretation of Nayler's trial regards Parliament's handling of the case and Cromwell's inaction as proof that Quakerism and liberty of conscience, not Nayler, were the main defendants.[378] Indeed, much to Bishop's dismay, the year 1657 brought hardship for all three.

CHAPTER SIX

Reading the Handwriting on the Wall: Bishop, Conscience, and the Fall of the Republic

AFTER THE CONCLUSION of Nayler's trial, Bishop suffered personal tragedy. In September 1657, Elizabeth Bishop delivered a son, Benoni, who died the next day. Exactly one year after the infant's birth, Elizabeth Bishop herself died, leaving Bishop alone to care for their three-year-old daughter.[379] In 1657 he published a lengthy defense of Quakerism, *The Throne of Truth*, a book he may have written while the House heard Nayler's testimony. The publication of this work marked a turning point in his Quaker activism.

Bishop's coordination of Bristol Quakerism and his work with Fox, Fell, and other prominent figures was enhanced by what soon emerged as a steady output of Quaker tracts. His work contains his evolving perception of religious truth, as well as testimonies and reports he received from his brethren. By at least 1657, traveling Quakers were sending him accounts of 'the Christian-like carriage of the Indians' in the New World who, unlike the harsh Dutch settlers, treated them with kindness.[380] His work reveals that Bishop's evolving Quakerism was rooted alongside his search for religious liberty. His tracts, especially those written after Nayler's trial and the legislation that followed, mourn the fact that this liberty was becoming increasingly remote.

In his 1657, *The Throne of Truth*, Bishop sought to justify Quaker principles and to counter the damage that the Nayler episode had done to the movement's image. The book, however, was presented as a rejoinder to the anti-Quaker accusations that had appeared in the Presbyterian minister Ralph Farmer's *Satan Inthron'd*. An avowed enemy of the Quakers, Farmer was present when the Bristol authorities examined Nayler in October 1656. Assuming the posture of an informed eyewitness, Farmer condemned what he regarded as the blasphemous actions of Nayler and his group. He named Bishop, Fox, and Nayler as prime examples of sectarian hypocrisy; and he argued that their failure to agree on spiritual matters demonstrated the incongruous, unsound nature of the Quaker movement. Referring to the Quakers as 'Satan's factors,' he charged that they bred destruction, 'confounding minister and ministry, word, churches, order, peace, civility, good manners ... truth itself, and all religion.'[381] Farmer argued that their central doctrine, the inner light, pretended to be the fountain of God's righteousness and truth. He reasoned, however, that the dissension between Nayler and his group, and Bishop, Fox, and their followers, invalidated the Quakers' claim to spiritual discernment. Farmer questioned how one could fail to see that they 'lyingly and hypocritically pretend to an infallibility.'[382]

In *The Throne of Truth*, Bishop sought to dismantle Farmer's credibility and the cogency of his arguments. In so doing, he hoped to clear the way for his vindication of Quakerism. He maintained that throughout the history of Christianity, temptation and sinful deeds had caused people to go 'out of truth ... (and make) a shipwreck of faith and good conscience.'[383] He conceded that Nayler had fallen victim to the temptation of the spirit that had 'darkened him,' and subsequently 'went out of truth in which light we believe and which light we follow after.'[384] Nonetheless, misguided actions—and here Bishop included Farmer's accusations as well as Nayler's erroneous ways of glorifying God—did nothing to devalue true Christian principles. Despite such apostasy, he maintained:

> the truth remaineth one and changed not
> ... For there is no lie of the truth nor in it
> is there any division ... and though an hour
> of darkness is come, for a trial to try the
> inhabitants of the earth ... [Yet] our God
> is one, and Christ is one, and the spirit is
> one, and the truth is one, and we all (who
> abide in truth are one ...)[385]

93

Bishop described the period during which he wrote *The Throne of Truth* as 'this day of the Lord's controversy of Sion.' Although he found it important to respond to Farmer's attack on the Quakers, his main concern was to protect the movement from Parliament's antitolerant attitude. In May 1656, in the wake of the Nayler episode, the second Protectorate Parliament, frequently called Nayler's Parliament, installed a new constitution, the Humble Petition and Advice. In contrast to the Instrument of Government, it more clearly defined the line between liberty and licentiousness. Consequently it outlawed many sectarian practices. While retaining the nominal protection that articles thirty-seven and thirty-eight of the Instrument had extended to radical sectaries, the Petition sought to silence the publishers of 'horrid blasphemies' and those whose practices they condemned for being 'licentious ... or profane ... under the profession of Christ.'[386] Aimed at forbidding heresy, in particular the Socinian doctrine of antitrinitarianism, and at punishing those who disturbed church services, the new constitution required that 'such as do openly revile them (godly ministers) or their assemblies, or disturb them in the worship or services ... to the dishonor of God, or scandal of good men, or breach the peace, may be punished according to law.'[387]

Parliament defined true Protestant Christian religion as that which is 'contained in the Holy Scriptures of the Old and New Testament,' and specified that no alternate form of religious certainty 'be held forth.' It also emphasized the co-equal nature of the Holy Trinity.[388] Aware of the Petition's antiheresy clauses, Bishop was careful to distinguish Quakerism from the most feared sect of his day, Socinianism. Socinian thought, grounded in the authority of Scripture and in Renaissance humanism that employed human reason as a source of religious truth, was a form of antitrinitarianism. As such it denied the doctrine of the trinity and the divinity of Jesus Christ. Viewed as murderous agents of the devil by their contemporaries, the Socinians were regarded as subversive anti-Christians who lacked moral or spiritual worth. One historian has commented that, in Reformation and post-Reformation Europe, 'when pens were often dipped in gall, the rise and spread of Socinianism was attended by unusual acrimony and hatred.'[389]

Unfortunately for the Quakers, the doctrine of the inner light appeared to be a denial of the historical Christ. Nayler's appearance, his ride into Bristol, and the adulation of his followers served to obscure the differences that in fact existed between the Quakers and the Socinians.[390] During Nayler's trial, as might be expected, Parliament made reference to the case of the Socinian John Biddle, whose antitrinitarian catechisms caused such alarm in 1654 that Parliament decided to burn his books and banish him to the Isle of Scilly.[391] In *The Throne of Truth*, Bishop carefully disassociated the Quakers from the Socinians. He explained the inner light as 'unchangeable truth,' the internalization of Christ's redeeming spirit. He described it as 'the voice and teaching of him who is given for a covenant of light to the Gentiles; the law written within the heart, the anointing which we hear and follow, which shows us when we go to the right hand or to the left.'[392] To protect the growing movement from anticipated attack, Bishop maintained that the inner light exalts rather than denies or diminishes the divinity of Christ.[393]

Farmer, he asserted, had committed 'high slander' when he accused the Quakers of denying the divine, redeeming power of the historical Jesus Christ. Bishop explained that Farmer had misrepresented the Quaker understanding of the inner light as 'never such words as ... (he) expressed came out of the people called Quakers' lips.'[394] The Quakers, he continued, 'Witness the Jesus Christ ... (who) was crucified at Jerusalem, and his resurrection and his blood, which cleanseth from all sin.'[395] Yet, despite the work of Bishop and other writers, fear of the Quakers seemed to grow rather than diminish.

The second Protectorate Parliament's curtailment of liberty of conscience has been linked with the increase in anti-Quaker violence and arrests that characterized the late 1650s.[396] Reay has catalogued the numerous instances when Quakers suffered harassment, beatings, and other forms of violence that were often provoked or exacerbated by those in authority.[397] In the period that followed the Nayler episode and the installation of The Humble Petition and Advice, Whitehall received numerous complaints concerning the harsh treatment of the local authorities.[398] Quakers were jailed for numerous reasons, like 'speaking' to a priest during church services or refusing to give hat honor or take an oath before a magistrate. Typically, the Quakers explained their arrests as the result of not 'pay(ing) tithes unto a man ... who teacheth for filthy lucre and minds earthly things,' or, as in the case of one Thomas Harris, who was imprisoned at Hartford, 'for setting up a paper of truth' against a priest.[399] Along with a plea for their brethren's innocence, one petition listed the names and various counties where Quakers had been detained. It stated:

> It may seem strange … (that) so many of our friends should be cast into prisons, there being few jails or houses of correction in England to which some of them have not been committed. And it is no less strange to us that such frequent and heavy sufferings for matters of conscience should come upon us and our brethren who for the most part have been instruments with thou and others for casting off that yoke of oppression which at the beginning of the late wars lay upon the honest people of this land.[400]

In the years that preceded his death, Oliver Cromwell continued to recognize the right of Englishmen to follow their own consciences in matters of religion. For those who exceeded the limits of the law, he preferred reformation to cruelty. Yet, despite his regard for religious liberty, he made it clear that he unequivocally rejected many of the radical sectaries' principles and practices. After the conclusion of the Nayler affair, he endorsed two additional bills, one an extended version of the Elizabethan Vagrancy Act and another designed to promote 'better observation of the Lord's Day.'[401] These bills, of course, jeopardized the safety of traveling Quakers whose consciences prompted them to spread the truth and to disrupt rather than attend, church services. However, to the chagrin of the religiously conservative Parliament, Cromwell withheld his approval of the bill for catechizing, which would have required ministers to preach from a designated text.[402]

Cromwell's religious policy during the last years of his life was complicated. On the one had, he expressed approval of the limits that Parliament placed on the radicals in 1656. Yet, as Worden has pointed out, these were laws that gave 'statutory protection to the people of God and at the same time [they] would have trapped Biddle and Nayler.'[403] It was also the case that Quakers who ran into trouble with local authorities occasionally found clemency at Whitehall. The Council of State, with the approval of Cromwell and, after his death in September 1658, with that of his son and successor, Richard, mitigated their misfortunes. But, as one historian has noted, 'The central government had little control over the local authorities who were hostile to the Quakers.'[404]

The uncertainty of the Quakers' safety apparently deepened Bishop's disenchantment with the political situation. The elusive search for liberty of conscience became the urgent, central focus of his writing between 1658 and the February 1660 return of the secluded members of the Long Parliament and anticipated restoration of Charles II.[405] On 9 September 1658, six days after Oliver Cromwell's death, Bishop wrote to Richard Cromwell, boldly cautioning the new Protector to "heed Him by whom kings reign and princes decree justice, the principle of God in thee, which moves to justice and to mercy.'[406] Bishop's appeal came at a time when disgruntled Quakers were addressing the Protector and his council concerning the treatment that their brethren 'received at the hands of those who claimed to be the champions of liberty of conscience.'[407] They enumerated the charges brought against their brethren and complained that the Quakers had been the worst victims of religious persecution since the reign of Queen Mary.[408]

Bishop hoped to persuade Richard Cromwell to treat the Quakers fairly in matters of 'judgment and justice,' and warned the new Protector that, if he refused to follow his internal spirit, he might soon be 'overturned.'[409] Bishop told him he could avert divine retribution if he reversed the suffering of those who were in jail for attending Quaker meetings, disrupting services, and refusing to pay tithes. Yet the Protector and the Parliament he summoned in January 1659 to raise revenues showed little concern for the Quakers' demands. On the contrary, the third Protectorate Parliament was irritated by a petition that the Quakers delivered to them on 6 April. *A Declaration to the Parliament* explained that the number of imprisoned Quakers had risen, and to ease their brethrens' suffering, the petitioners requested permission to exchange places with those in jail. When the appeal was discussed in Parliament, however, it became clear that most MPs considered the petitioners and their brethren to be troublesome fanatics. They chided them to have more respect for their superiors and ordered them to return to their counties. They were told that henceforth they were to obey the justices and the laws they were charged with enforcing.[410]

During the following year, however, the twists and turns of political events made the situation hopeful for religious radicals. Encouraged by the political events of early 1659, Bishop served the Quakers as a valuable spokesperson. Now 'the most prominent of the early ... [Quakers] in Bristol,' he solicited those in power to initiate an era of religious liberty.[411] In 1659 and early 1660 Bishop wrote numerous petitions to former military and political associates in London, including Fleetwood and Vane. These men had come to the center of affairs in the spring of 1659 in response to the cries of dissatisfied radicals and republicans who called for a return to 'the good old cause,' the cause of political and religious reform.

In April, with the backing of junior officers and sectaries who resented the 1657 attack on religious liberty and the attempt to make Cromwell king, a group of officers, including Desborough and Fleetwood, forced Richard Cromwell to dissolve his Parliament. Shortly thereafter, Cromwell stepped down as Protector, and the Commonwealth was restored.[412]

The Quakers saw this as the first real opportunity for reform since the days of the Nominated Parliament. They remarked, 'Things in the city generally are well, and truth is of a dominion ... a mighty thirst and desire and openness are in many people in most places, especially since the change of government.'[413] The Quakers' renewed hope that God's cause would now be vindicated occasioned a noticeable increase in publications. Smith has listed 180 Quaker tracts for 1659, a marked increase over the 75 for 1658 and 90 for 1656.[414] Maclear has commented that, 'the government was continuing to seek a strong basis of support among the sects, believing that this was the last chance to find that stable order which was the only effective barrier to the Stuart restoration.'[415] Bishop too, as Cole has noted, 'at once recognized the opportunity [that] it [the dismissal of Richard Cromwell's Parliament] afforded.[416] Bishop looked to the army as God's chosen instrument of reform, and until the eve of the king's restoration, he continued to press the officers to effect extensive religious reform. He urged them to abolish tithes and a paid clergy, and to reverse the limitations set by the Humble Petition and Advice. He began this effort on 27 April, when he petitioned the Council of Officers on behalf of the Quakers, especially those who were imprisoned after refusing to pay tithes.

Mindful that attempts at reform had failed in recent years, Bishop outlined some guidelines that would safeguard the deliverance of the good old cause. He presented the army officers with a twelve-point program that warned them away from lawyers and 'soul murdering and conscience bending clergymen,' whom he regarded as the perverters of righteousness.[417] He cautioned the officers to entrust positions of power only to those who promote 'the spirit of the cause.'[418] Distrustful of recent Parliaments and fearful of lawyers whose disdain of the sectaries had proved them enemies of conscience, Bishop implored the army to 'make some examples of those in Parliament, court, council [and] army who sought to destroy a reformation of law.'[419]

Bishop reminded the army officers that their April dissolution of Parliament had cleared the way for a return to their original principles, the 'virgin declaration[s]' that they had outlined in both their November 1648 Remonstrance of St. Albans and the January 1649 Settlement of the Nation. The January 1649 proposal had barred Parliament from 'imposing in matters of religion or conscience, things spiritual or evangelical, or granting it (in the least) to any part of the public interest.'[420] He reminded the officers that, upon the creation of the Commonwealth, Parliament was to be entrusted with the preservation, 'altering repealing and declaring of laws ... in all natural and civil things, but not concerning things spiritual or evangelical.'[421]

Evidently Bishop thought that Parliament should act as a noninterfering guardian in spiritual matters. Parliament's function would be to abolish laws that threatened the freedom of the sectaries and to punish ministers and magistrates, or any interfering party, who sought to deprive them of this basic right. He maintained that 'the famous Long Parliament ... [had] managed and carried through the good old cause,' and he implored the army to summon their surviving members.[422] Like other Quaker leaders, Bishop had denounced the effects of the moderate Protectorate Parliaments whose antitolerant attitudes had jeopardized the movement's safety. Yet his strong republican sentiments and association with Whitehall politicians may have distinguished him from the great number of Quakers who were indifferent when the Rump Parliament was recalled on 7 May.[423] Nonetheless, for whatever reasons, unlike the vast majority of his brethren, Bishop was hopeful that the Rump would support liberty of conscience.

Soon after their 7 May reinstatement, Bishop enlisted the Rump's support in his work on behalf of the Quakers. In so doing, he identified their disappointment with his own. In early May Bishop wrote to Parliament and discussed the 'disgraceful six-year captivity of the Commonwealth.'[424] In his *Mene Tekel*, he discussed the problems he had encountered at Bristol and Whitehall during the intervening years. He wrote:

> Since the interruption [the 20 April 1653 dissolution] what I have done and suffered I speak not. My life is given me for a prey (after all the secret huntings of my blood) [Yet] … my integrity is with the Lord, that from the beginning [the outbreak of the wars] I have never betrayed nor acted against my principle … neither valuing my life nor what I had, in return to the Commonwealth, so I have continued to this day, mourning with them that mourn and weeping for them who wept for it.[425]

The recent Parliaments' unwillingness to outlaw tithes and a paid ministry, Bishop warned the Rump, was a mistake they must not repeat. Between 1653 and 1659 approximately one thousand court cases had resulted from the opposition to tithes.[426] In light of such measures, Bishop maintained that Oliver Cromwell's Parliaments had 'set their foot on liberty of conscience.' Now, in his estimation, it was the task of the restored Rump to avoid 'judgment … [from] God and to plead the cause of his people.'[427]

Shortly after their recall, the Rump displayed a friendly attitude toward those who had been imprisoned for conscience. They had released several prisoners, including Nayler, and accepted petitions that listed names of Quakers and other 'moderate' men who might replace 'persecuting' magistrates.[428] Bishop was encouraged when Parliament formed a committee to examine tithe cases. After conducting an investigation, the committee filed a report that described the harsh prison conditions. They also issued orders for certain justices to release their prisoners.[429] Indeed, for a brief time, Bishop noted that it seemed likely that the Rump would outlaw the collection of tithes.

However, to Bishop's disappointment, Parliament failed to take the necessary steps to prevent future arrests. Apparently disinterested in the matter of imprisoned Quakers, they pursued it no further. Consequently, Quaker arrests continued, perhaps even increased. Since the issue of tithes was the most pressing concern for Quakers during the summer of 1659, Parliament's failure to outlaw their 'utter taking away' greatly added to the dismay that Bishop began to reexperience.[430]

Religious liberty was further diminished by the army officers' 12 May address to Parliament. At Wallingford House, Fleetwood's London residence, the officers drafted recommendations for what they regarded as an equitable religious settlement. Bishop saw articles seven and eight of the officers' petition as a fatal blow to religious liberty, the good old cause. These articles supported collection of tithes to maintain a university-trained ministry. It also specified that 'a godly, faithful, and gospel-preaching ministry be everywhere encouraged, countenanced, and maintained.'[431] It reconfirmed the provision in the Humble Petition and Advice that denied liberty of conscience to those who 'practice or hold forth licentiousness or profaneness under religion.'[432]

Bishop was fearful of the additional restrictions upon conscience that might result from the army's decision to deliver custody of religion into Parliament's hands. Mindful that the Quakers' safety was threatened by an environment that was hostile to free expression, Bishop chastized the army for perpetuating 'the slavery and slaughter' that had begun with the former Parliament's installation of the Humble Petition and Advice. One major source of his concern was the fact that the document made it possible for magistrates to detain those who had caused a disturbance because of something they had written or printed.[433] Bishop reminded the officers how Oliver Cromwell had trampled 'on the cause ... [namely, by] asserting coercive power in them [Parliament] in matters of religion, and of conscience.'[434] Moreover, he remarked, the 12 May Address increased the control of 'vengeful' justices, since it broadened the definition of what constituted 'an actual disturbance' of a religious service.[435] According to Bishop, the handwriting was on the wall for all to see that the army had carelessly turned the 'good old cause into a bad new one.'[436]

There were also signs that the republic was in jeopardy. Relations were strained between Parliament and the army. The unpaid soldiers could not be expected to feel warmly toward Parliament and were 'in the mood to listen to any plan which promised ... pay.'[437] According to Woolrych, 'The Rump certainly did not regard itself as the 'parliamentary agent' of the army grandees whom it soon proceeded to cut down to size.'[438] Parliament proposed that, in the future, the Speaker of the House assign army commissions. The army interpreted this move as a Parliamentary conspiracy to arbitrarily cast out anyone who opposed them. They feared parties would be 'made, headed and encouraged by diverse members sitting in Parliament.'[439]

Furthermore, any chance of cooperation between the army and Parliament was destroyed by the army's Derby Petition. Along with other recommendations, the petition advised Parliament to accept the army's 12 May recommendations, since they were the only visible plan for civil and religious reform. Allegedly in an effort to promote an atmosphere of good will, Fleetwood showed the petition to Vane and to his fellow MPs, Arthur Haselrig and Richard Salway, outspoken republicans who had been excluded from the Protectorate Parliaments. On 22 September, Haselrig presented this matter to the House. Protesting that the army meant to interfere where they had no business, numerous MPs criticized the officers' intentions, denounced the petition, and spoke of sending one of its proponents, John Lambert, briefly to the tower.[440]

Throughout the series of setbacks that began to plague the faltering Commonwealth, Bishop and his Quaker associates in Bristol remained unwavering in their support. In July, Bishop's collaborators on *The Cry of Blood*, Thomas Gouldney, Dennis Hollister, Edward Pyott, Henry Roe, and their fellow Bristolian Thomas Speed, accepted appointments to serve as militia commissioners from Bristol. The Quaker support of the Commonwealth was so conspicuous that the Earl of Clarendon commented that Parliament 'had put the whole militia of the kingdom into the hands of sectaries, persons of no degree or quality, and notorious for some new tenets in religion and some for barbarity exercised upon the king's party.'[441]

In August there was an insurrection in Cheshire and south Lancashire led by the royalist Sir George Booth. Booth, who survived his capture, wrote a tract which showed that religion and 'the gentry's traditional position,' were the main concerns of the insurgents. Apparently, fear of radical sectaries, and the fact that so many of them had received militia commissions, provoked a conservative backlash that resulted in the return of the king.[442] Ironically, it seems that the Quakers who received commissions were reluctant to engage in combat. Alexander Parker, a prominent Quaker, considered the possibility of fighting a cause of great concern and sought Fox's advice in the matter.[443]

After Lambert and his troops defeated Booth, and the Commonwealth seemed momentarily safe from the threat of rebellion, the animosity between the army and Parliament deepened. Parliament continued to press for measures that would secure their control of military affairs; in turn, the army antagonized Parliament with talk of religious reform. By the time Parliament had rejected a plan for toleration that was allegedly proposed by Vane,[444] it had become increasingly clear to Bishop that religious reform would not be forthcoming. In fact, between their 7 May recall and their 13 October dismissal the Rump had failed to produce one piece of religious reform.

After Lambert's 13 October dismissal of the Rump, Bishop continued to urge the army to take the lead in reform. He wrote the army officers and commented that their dismissal of Parliament had been a 'desparate necessity [that] had forced the just hand of the Lord.'[445] According to him, Parliament had 'misused' their day, and he beseeched the army to avoid a similar tragedy.[446]

After the October dismissal of the Rump, however, there was a noticeable split in the army between Lambert's troops and those under the avowed enemy of the Quakers, General George Monck. As Monck's forces began a southward march from Scotland and listened to cries for 'a full and free Parliament,' Bishop expressed his disillusionment. In November he wrote a letter to a member of the London militia, possibly Vane, and declined what appears to be a suggestion to serve as a commissioner.[447] His refusal, it must be noted, was not grounded on any pacifist beliefs that were yet to emerge. He was not interested in coming to London, he explained, because 'The General Council of the Officers have not laid the basis of their government in justice and righteousness, but in the mixtures of corruption and bad interests.'[448] Their neglect to discontinue the system of tithes, and their failure to broaden the limits of religious liberty, Bishop remarked, were evidence that they had fallen 'under the spirit' that had risen up against them. This spirit had thwarted religious reform, he explained, and was embodied in any faction—Presbyterian, Independent, royalist, or otherwise—that prevented the securing of liberty of conscience.[449]

Vane himself missed the chance to effect religious reform. Although he was an important member of the Committee of Safety that governed from the 13 October dismissal to the December return of the Rump, it has been noted that 'no strenuous efforts were made to gratify Quakerism in any of its desires. The fact of the matter was that the army grandees were more concerned with personal aggrandizement and opportunism than the triumph of the good old cause.'[450] Consequently, like other Quakers, by November 1659 Bishop saw little chance that the Committee of Safety would effect any reforms. However disappointing it may have been, it was clear that a national church with a university-trained ministry, preaching the gospel and being paid by tithes, was the way that the church would continue to be structured. Recognizing the gravity of the situation, Bishop placed increasing emphasis on inward security, explaining that the Commonwealth would soon be replaced by the reign of Christ.[451]

The Royalist sentiment in Bristol—charged by recent national events—provoked anti-Quaker violence. On 2 February, the day Monck and his army entered London, Bristol apprentices began a week-long demonstration. They virtually paralyzed the city and desisted only after a troop of horsemen were sent into the city to suppress them.[452] During the course of the riots, apprentices vented their anger against the Quakers. On 6 February, they came armed to the house of Bishop's associate Edward Pyott; and two days later, Hollister, Pyott, and visiting preacher William Dewsbury were startled by a group of rioters as they walked to a meeting at Bishop's house.[453] Mortimer has suggested that a local merchant, Richard Ellsworth, was the 'main instigator' of the riots. Ellsworth allegedly harbored hostile intentions against the mayor, the Baptists, and the Quakers.[454] Mortimer has commented that, in early 1660, the royalist 'outlook' and anti-Quaker sentiment in Bristol was so strong that no Quakers were nominated to serve in the city militia when it was formed in March.[455]

Thus, during the winter months of 1660 the government that had failed to secure liberty of conscience was unable to withstand the pressure of its own internal divisions and the growing tide of royalism. A recent commentator noted how it was the general's lack of vision and politican acumen, not the royalist forces', that brought about the army's defeat.[456] After an eleven-year interruption, the surviving MPs who had sought to continue negotiations for a settlement with Charles I retook their seats in February 1660. The imminent return of the king, Bishop knew, boded disaster for the sectaries and for the future of religious reform. Consequently, the passing of the republic would root him more securely into the kingdom of Christ. In tones that were reminiscent of the disenchantment that had turned him toward Quakerism after his 1654 return to Bristol, in February 1660 Bishop offered spiritual reassurance to the divided army. He told them:

> Be not ye troubled, neither faint in your minds, nor be offended nor stumbled, but turn in hither, return—come to the immortal in you which witnesseth for God, which gives you the sense of those things and shows unto you all that ye have done ... man's day is done but the Lord's day is come.[457]

In the years that followed, after the monarchy, House of Lords, and Anglican church had been restored to their traditional place in English society, it is interesting to think how often Bishop must have repeated this sentiment. Henceforth this soldier and his developing ideology of religious liberty would retreat more deeply into the 'kingdom that cannot be shaken.'

EPILOGUE

THE PERIOD BETWEEN Charles II's May 1660 return from Breda and Bishop's death in November 1668 proved extremely dangerous for the Quakers. Arrests, fines, and the threat of banishment for violating the laws against nonconformity continued until the passing of the Toleration Act in 1689. Like other Quakers and sectarians, Bishop wrote 'warnings' to the king, instructing him to rule in the principle of truth and ease the sufferings of the religiously oppressed. His *To Thee Charles Stuart King of England* argues that, like Moses, King Charles must make it his duty to safeguard God's people from the laws that had been made by those who sought to destroy them. Providence had restored the king to his father's throne. Now in recompense for God's benevolence, Bishop urged Charles II to secure legislation that would guarantee liberty of conscience. He warned that if unjust laws came to characterise his reign, God would punish the present king as he had 'the other chaffe before thee.'[458]

    The possibility of any such liberty soon dissolved as the king's ministers refused to prepare a bill with the provisions that one historian recently described as 'the hope of liberty for tender consciences … [that the king had] so shrewdly—and probably sincerely—promised at Breda.'[459] In Bristol the magistrates now had the unequivocal support of Whitehall against the Quakers. The first wave of arrests followed the January 1661 rising of London Fifth Monarchists. In the year that followed, 186 Bristol Quakers—including Bishop—were arrested, a number far exceeding total arrests during the Commonwealth period in that city. Recently, Jonathan Barry has discussed how the Bristol magistrates exaggerated the extent of nonconformity, 'claiming that half or even two-thirds of Bristolians were sectarians or fanatics, when clearly the figures were much lower.'[460] These inflated numbers

106

undoubtably reflect the city fathers' fear of subversion and concern that disruption would adversely affect their expanding mercantile interests. The second wave of persecution followed the passing of the 1662 Quaker Act, which made subject to arrest those who refused to take an oath or met in groups of five or more. On one occasion when Bishop and Dennis Hollister were brought before the magistrates, they told them that 'they might as well think to keep the Sun from shining, or the Tide from flowing, as to think to hinder the Lord's people from meeting.'[461]

Bishop's ties completely severed from Whitehall politics, his advocacy for the Quakers during the last eight years of his life was centered in Bristol, where he wrote over twenty tracts, including *New England Judged*, one of the Quaker histories of persecution in Puritan Boston mentioned in Hawthorne's *The Scarlet Letter*.[462] A future study will demonstrate how, admist the turmoil of the anti-Quaker legislation and the cultural climate of Restoration England, Bishop combined natural reason and the more quiet form of Quakerism that several of his brethren had been following since the 1650s. His later writings, progressively move past securing secular approval to explaining conscience in metaphysical terms and advocating passive resistance. As his ideas evolved, the Parliamentary soldier turned Quaker explained how this quiet endurance sustains the spirit which 'cannot be reach't ... by force and violence, since, unlike the body and other corporeal matter, it belongs to the immortal realm.'[463]

NOTES

1 See Christopher Hill, *The Experience of Defeat: Milton and Some Contemporaries* (New York: Penguin Books, 1984).

2 Barry Reay, *The Quarkers and the English Revolution,* (New York: St. Martin's Press, 1985), Chapter 4.

3 J.H. Hexter, "The Problem of the Presbyterian Independents," *American Historical Review,* xliv (1938- 39): 29-49; G. Yule, *The Independents in the English Civil War* (Cambridge: Cambridge University Press, 1958); D. Underdown, "The Independents Reconsidered," *Journal of British Studies,* iii (1964), 57-84; G. Yule, "Independents and Revolutionaries," *Ibid.,* vii (1968): 11-31; Underdown, "The Independents Again," *Ibid.,* vii (1968): 83-93.

4 V. Pearl, "'The Royal Independents' in the English Civil War," *Transactions of the Royal Historical Society,* 5th series, xviii (1968): 69-96.

5 C. Hill, *The Experience of Defeat,* 17, 20, 133.

6 Joseph W. Martin, "The Pre-Quaker Writings of George Bishop," *Quaker History,* Vol. 74, Number 2, (Fall 19785): 20.

7 D. Hirst, *Authority and Conflict in England 1603-1658* (London: Edward Arnold Publishers, 1986), 167.

8 L. Solt, *Saints in Arms: Puritanism and Democracy in Cromwell's Army* (Stanford: Stanford University Press, 1959), chapter one.

9 *The Humble Desires and Proposals of the Private Agitators of Colonel Hewson's Regiment* (London: Printed for I.C., 1647).

10 Hill, *The Experience of Defeat* 21-22; Nigel Smith, *Literature and Revolution in England 1640-1660.* (New Haven: Yale University Press, 1994), chapter one.

11 T. Hall, *Vindiciae Literarum* (London, 1655), 215: quoted in C. Hill, *The World Turned Upside Down: Radical Ideas during the Puritan Revolution* (Middlesex, England: Penguin Books, 1984), 373.

12 W.K. Jordan, *Men of Substance: A Study of the Thought of Two English Revolutionaries* (New York: Octagon Books, 1967), 127.

13 *Ibid.*

14 A.P. Woolrich, *Printing in Bristol* (Bristol: The Historical Association, 1985), 1-2; Smith, *Literature and Revolution,* 30; for a discussion on consorship during the period, see Lois Potter, *Secret Rites and Secret Writings: Royalist Literature 1641-1660.* (Cambridge: Cambridge University Press, 1989), chapter one.

15 R. Goertz, "To Plant the Pleasant Fruit of Freedom: Consciousness, Politics and Community in Digger and Early Quaker Thought" (Ph.D. dissertation, City University of New York Graduate Center, 1977).

16 C.H. Firth (ed), *The Clarke Papers, Selections from the Papers of William Clarke, Secretary to the Council of the Army, 1647-1649, and to General Monck and the*

Commanders of the Army in Scotland, 1651-1660 (London: The Camden Society, 1891), Vol. I, 340; A.L. Morton, *The World of the Ranters* (London: The Camelot Press, 1970), 64-68.

[17] D. Underdown, *Pride's Purge: Politics in the Puritan Revolution* (Oxford: The Clarendon Press, 1971), esp. chapter eight; A.H. Woolrych, *Soldiers and Statesmen: The General Council of the Army and Its Debates, 1647-1648* (Oxford: The Clarendon Press, 1987), 330-31, 336-37.

[18] A.H. Woolrych, *England without a King 1649-1660* (London and New York: Methuen, 1983), 14.

[19] *Acts and Ordinances of the Interregnum 1642-1660*, C.H. Firth and R.S. Rait (eds.) (London: His Majesty's Stationery Office, 1911), Vol. I, 582-609.

[20] *Ibid.*, Vol. I, 1133-36.

[21] Underdown, *Pride's Purge*, 129.

[22] W.K. Jordan, *The Development of Religious Toleration in England: Attainment of the Theory and Accommodation in Thought and Institutions* (1640-1660), Vol. III (Cambridge, Ma.: Harvard Univ. Press, 1938), 119-34.

[23] G. Bishop, *Mene Tekel* (London: Thomas Brewster, 1659), 37; Hill, *The Experience of Defeat*, 17.

[24] R. Bauman, *Let Your Words Be Few: Symbolism of Speaking and Silence among Seventeenth-Century Quakers* (Cambridge: Cambridge University Press, 1983), 84.

[25] George Bishop, *A Manifesto Declaring (London, 1665); Supplement to the Quarterly Meeting of Bristol and Somersetshire Burials 1659-1832*, SF/R1/6; *Supplement to the Quarterly Meeting of Bristol and Somersetshire Births 1659-1832*, SF/R1/2; Public Record Office, *Monthly Meeting of the Society of Friends of Bristol and Somersetshire Burials 1655-1779*, RG 6/666, 1, 2, 3, 12: *Monthly Meeting of the Society of Friends of Bristol and Somersetshire Births 1655-1779*, RG 6/1453, 3, 7.

[26] Gerald Aylmer, *The State's Servants: The Civil Service of the English Republic 1649-1660* (London and Boston: Routledge and Kegan Paul, 1973), 272-74; W.A. Cole, 'The Quakers and Politics, 1652-1660,' unpublished dissertation, Cambridge University, 1955; J. William Frost, 'George Bishop,' in *Biographical Dictionary of British Radicals in the Seventeenth Century* R. Greaves and R. Zaller, eds. (Sussex, Eng.: Harvester Press, 1982) Vol. I., 67; Joseph W. Martin, 'The Pre-Quaker Writings of George Bishop,' 20-27; Russell S. Mortimer, 'Quakerism in Seventeenth Century Bristol,' unpublished M.A. thesis, University of Bristol, 1946.

[27] Cole, "The Quakers and Politics, 1652-1660,"326; Hill, *The Experience of Defeat*, 129, 132.

[28] H. R. Plomer, *A Dictionary of the Booksellers and Printers Who Were at Work in England, Scotland and Ireland from 1641-1667* (London: Printed for the Bibliographical Society, 1907), 24, 193.

[29] Joseph Foster, *Amumni Oxonienses: The Members of the University of Oxford 1500-1714, Their Parentage, Birthplace and Year of Birth, With a Record of*

Their Degrees Being the Matriculated Register of the University (Oxford: Parker and Company, 1888) Early Series A-D; John Venn and J.A. Venn, compilers, *The Book of Matriculation and Degrees: A Catalogue of Those Who Have Been Matriculated or Been Admitted to Any Degree in the University of Cambridge from 1544-1659* (Cambridge: Cambridge University Press, 1913).

[30] Jonathan Barry, 'Seventeenth Century Bristol,' in Barry Reay, ed., *Popular Culture in Seventeenth Century England* (New York: St. Martin's Press, 1985); Nicholas Carlisle, *A Concise Dictionary of the Endowed Grammar Schools in England and Wales* (London: Baldwin and Cardock and Joy, 1818), Vol. II., 404-11; Jean Vanes, *Education and Apprenticeship in Sixteenth Century Bristol* (Bristol: The Bristol Branch of the Historical Association, 1982) 12-13.

[31] Bristol Records Office, *Burgess Book 1607-1659*, 50, 377.

[32] J. Besse, *A Collection of the Sufferings of the People Called Quakers*, (London: Luke Hinde, 1753), 42-3, 45, 48-50; Bishop *A Manifesto*, 28; Bristol Record Office, *Supplement of the Quarterly Meeting of Bristol and Somersetshire, Births 1653-1784*, SF/R1/2, Book 1507,3, 7; *Quarterly Meeting of Bristol and Somersetshire Burials, 1651-1837*: SF/R1/5, Book 123, 1-2; Public Record Office, Probated Will of George Bishop, PRO Prob. 12/45, 43.

[33] R.S. Mortimer (ed.) *The Minutes Books of the Men's Meeting of the Society of Friends in Bristol 1667-1686* (Bristol Record Society, 1971, 58-59.

[34] D.H. Sacks presents a good appraisal of the relationship between mercantile wealth and politics in Bristol, while explaining how royal patronage occasionally found it expedient to interfere in local affairs. D.H. Sacks 'The Corporate Town and the English State: Bristol's "Little Businesses" 1625-1641,' *Past and Present*, 110, (Feb. 1986): 69-105; for an extended discussion, see his *The Widening Gate: Bristol and the Atlantic Economy 1450-1700*. (Berkeley: Univ. of California Press, 1991).

[35] Bishop, *A Manifesto Declaring*, 10.

[36] G. Fox, *The Journal of George Fox, Edited from the Manuscript* (Cambridge: Cambridge University Press, 1911) Vol. I., 464. A number of future Quakers were relatives or married to relatives of Robert Yeamans. These relations of Elizabeth Canne Bishop were among George Bishop's closest friends and associates in Bristol. This group included Thomas Speed, one of Bishop's collaborators on *The Cry of Blood*, who married Yeaman's widow. The Quaker Elizabeth Yeamans, most probably one of the step-children who Speed introduced to Quakerism, was the wife of Judge John Haggett, Bishop's close associate. G. Fox *The Journal of George Fox*, Vol. I., 231, 363.

[37] Sacks, 'The Corporate Town and the English State,' 91, 96.

[38] Barry, 'Bristol,' 61; Patrick McGrath, *Merchants and Merchandise in Seventeenth Century Bristol* (Bristol: Bristol Record Society, 1952); Sacks, *Ibid.*, 76-85.

[39] Alfred Beaven, comp., *Bristol Lists: Municipal and Miscellaneous* (Bristol: T.D. Taylor, Sons and Hawkins, 1899); George Bishop et al., *The Cry of Blood and Herod* (London: Giles Calvert, 1656), 19, 63-64, 76, 89; Robert Hayden, ed., *The Records of a Church of Christian Bristol, 1640-1687* (Bristol: Bristol Record Society, 1974), 75.

40 Friends Historical Library, Swarthmore College; William Penn to Robert Vickris, 8th day, 4th month 1681, *Penn Manuscript*, Braithwaite, *The Second Period of Quakerism*, 107; Craig Horle's 'Death of a Felon: Richard Vickris and the Elizabeth Conventicle Act,' *Quaker History*, Vol. 76, Fall 1987 #2: 95-107, discusses Vickris' legal difficulties.

41 Somerset Record Office, *Friends Birth and Burial Records*, SF/R1/2; 84, 122. Thomas Bishop Vickris to Caleb Dickinson, July to September 1739, Dickinson Manuscript, DD/DN 199.

42 See especially: G. Bishop, *Jesus Christ the Same Today* (London: Giles Calvert 1656; London: Thomas Brewster, 1659) *The Warnings of the Lord* (London, Bristol: M. Inman and R. Moon, 1660).

43 *Ibid.*, Bishop, Warnings, 3-6.

44 Bishop, *Mene Tekel*, 4.

45 Patrick McGrath, *The Civil War in Bristol* (Bristol: Bristol Branch of the Historical Association,1981), 10-46; For a discussion of the pre-war religious animosity in England as a whole, see N. Tyacke 'Puritanism, Arminianism and Counter-Revolution,' *The Origins of the Civil War*, C. Russell (ed.) (New York: Harper & Row, 1973).

46 Richard Robinson, *Sieges of Bristol during the Civil War*, (Bristol: Leech and Taylor, 1968), 6-9.

47 Sacks, 'The Corporate Town,' 97.

48 Robinson, *Sieges of Bristol*, 10-12.

49 W. Adams, *Adam's Chronicle of Bristol*, (ed.) F.F. Fox (Bristol, 1910), 256: quoted in Sacks, 'The Corporate Town,' 77.

50 Leo Solt, review of *Authority and Conflict*, by Derek Hirst, in *Church History*, p. 56 No. 3, (September 1987), 406-06.

51 Robinson, *Sieges of Bristol*, 10-12.

52 D. Underdown, *Somerset in the Civil War and Interregnum*, (London: David and Charles: Newton Abbott, 1973), 113.

53 *Ibid.*

54 *A True Relation of the Storming of Bristol and the Taking of the Town, Castle, Forts, Ordinances, Ammunition and Arms by Sir Thomas Fairfax's Army on Thursday the 16th of Sept, 1645* (London: Printed for Edward Husbands, Sept. 1645) BL E 301 (5).

55 Bishop, *A Manifesto*, 1.

56 *Lt. General Oliver Cromwell's Letter of the House of Commons of All the Particulars of the Taking of City of Bristol* (London: Edward Husbands, Sept. 18, 1648) BL E 84 (31).

57 *The Petition of the City of Bristol for Peace Presented to the King at Oxford, With His Majestie's Answer*, Bristol, 1643.

58 *Ibid.*

59 *Ibid.*

[60] Bishop, *A Manifesto*, 1.

[61] G. Bishop, *A More Particular and Exact Relation of the Victory*, (London: R. Cotes, 1645) 1-2; A.H. Woolrych, *Battles of the Civil War, Marston Moor, Naseby and Preston* (London: B.T. Batsford Ltd., 1961) 111-139, 192.

[62] *Ibid.* Bishop, 2-3.

[63] C.E. Philips, *Cromwell's Captains* (Freeport: Books for Libraries Press, 1938), 138.

[64] Bishop, *A More Particular*, 1-3.

[65] Bishop, *Mene Tekel*, 35.

[66] Woolrych, *Battles of the Civil War*, 139.

[67] Woolrych, *Soldiers and Statesmen*, Chapters II and III.

[68] *Ibid.*

[69] A good discussion of the agitation in the army can be found in: C. Hill, *The World Turned Upside Down*, Chapter Four. Mark Kishlanksy, 'Consensus Politics and the Structure of the Debate at Putney,' in *The Origins of Anglo-American Radicalism*, eds. James R. Jacob and Margaret C. Jacob, (London: George Allen and Unwin, 1984) A.L. Morton, *The World of the Ranters*, 63; Solt, *Saints*, 6-24; Austin Woolrych, *Soldiers and Statesmen* (Oxford: Clarendon Press, 1987), Chapter Three.

[70] Hirst, *Authority and Conflict*, 277-78, 286; Solt, *Saints in Arms*, 16-19; Woolrych, *Soldiers and Statesmen*, 215-217, 279-86; Zagorin, *Political Thought*, 35-42.

[71] Bishop, *A Manifesto*, 1.

[72] *Ibid.*, 2.

[73] *Ibid.*

[74] Blair Worden, 'Providence and Politics in Cromwellian England,' *Past and Present*, 109, (1985): 91.

[75] C.H. Firth, *The Clarke Papers* Vol. I, 340.

[76] J. Rushworth, *Historical Collections of Private Passages of State, Weighty Passages in Law* (London: D. Brown, 1721-1722), Vol. VII., 945. Woodhouse, *Puritanism and Liberty*, 81, 438-39, 1071; BL E 555 (13), 5-6; John Saltmarsh, *Friends Raised from the Grave* (London: Gills Calvert, 1649).

[77] Underdown, *Pride's Purge*, 84-88.

[78] C.H. Firth, *The Clarke Papers*, Vol. I., 440-41, 416.

[79] *Ibid.*, 383.

[80] *Ibid.*

[81] *Ibid.*

[82] Hill, *The Experience of Defeat*, 33.

[83] Bishop, *Mene Tekel*, 5-6.

[84] G. Bishop, *To Thee Charles Stuart King of England* (Bristol, 1660), 5.

[85] *Cal. S.P. Dom.* (1649-1650), 459.

86 Aylmer, *The State's Servants*, 204, 398-99.

87 Underdown, *Pride's Purge,* esp. chapter 6.

88 Bishop, *Mene Tekel,* 4.

89 K. Wrightson *English Society 1580-1680* (New Brunswick: Rutgers Univ. Press, 1982.

90 Sacks, "The Corporate Town," 53-61.

91 Underdown, *Revel, Riot and Rebellion: Popular Politics and Culture in England 1603-1660* (Oxford Univ. Press, 1985), 210, 236; 53-61.

92 *Original Letters and Papers of State Addressed to Oliver Cromwell Concerning the Affairs of Great Britain from the Year 1649-1658. Found among the Political Collections of John Milton.* J. Nickolls (ed.) (London: William Bowyer, 1743), 49; George Bishop, *A Modest Check to Part of a Most Scandalous Libel,* (London, 1650) 6.

93 J. Charles Fox, *The Royal Forests of England,* (London: Methuen and Company, 1905) 274-81.

94 D. Underdown, 'The Chalk and the Cheese: Contrasts among English Clubmen,' *Past and Present,* 85, (November 1979): 38.

95 C.H. Firth and R.S. Rait for the Statute Law Committee, *Acts and Ordinances of the Interregnum 1642-1660* (Holmes Bea., Fla.: Wm. Gaunt and Sons, Inc., 1973), Vol. I., p. 1125, citing *The Journal of the House of Lords,* X. 211.

96 *The Revolt of the Provinces: Conservatives and Radicals in the English Civil War.* (London: G. Allen and Unwin, 1976), 81; D. Underdown, *Revel, Riot and Rebellion,* 211.

97 Ibid., *Morrill,* 204.

98 *Cal of S.P. Dom* (1649-1650) 443-44, 447; Martin, 'The Pre-Quaker Writings of George Bishop,' 23.

99 Bishop, *A Modest Check,* 5.

100 F. Raab, *The English Face of Machiavelli: A Changing Interpretation 1500-1700,* (London: Routledge and Kegan Paul, 1965), 102-06, 117.

101 *Ibid.,* 106.

102 Bishop, *A Modest Check,* 5-6.

103 *Ibid.*

104 BL E 94 (24), *A Declaration and Ordinance of the Lords and Commons,* (London: Edward Husbands, 1643), 1-15.

105 Morrill, *The Revolt of the Provinces,* 184.

106 D. Underdown, *Royalist Conspiracy,* (New Haven: Yale Univ. Press, 1960), 7-8.

107 *Ibid., A Declaration and Ordinance,* 2.; *Index to the Royalist Composition Papers,* W.P.W. Phillimore (ed.) (London: Charles J. Clark, Lincoln's Inn Fields, 1889), 5.

108 Accounts of how political change was received in London and the provinces can be found in Morrill, *Revolt of the Provinces;* Underdown, *Revel, Riot, and Rebellion;* and Wrightson, *English Society.*

[109] Bishop, *A Manifesto*, 4.

[110] Wrightson, *English Society*, 51 and his note 9.

[111] *Ibid.*; *Milton State Papers*, 55.

[112] *Cal. S. P. Dom.* (1649-1650), 149, 443, 447, 471.

[113] Martin, 'The Pre-Quaker Writings of George Bishop,' 21.

[114] Bishop, *A Manifesto Declaring*, 17-18.

[115] Quoted in: *Records Relating to the Society of Merchant Venturers of the City of Bristol in the Seventeenth Century.* P. McGrath (ed.) (Bristol: Bristol Records Society's Publications, 1952).

[116] *Cal. S. P. Dom.* (1650), 339.

[117] Bishop, *A Manifesto*, 8.

[118] *Dictionary of Nationaly Biography*, L. Stephen and S. Lee (eds.) (Edward Winslow), Vol. 21, (Oxford: Oxford University Press, 1882), 672-74.

[119] *Index Nominum to the Royalist Composition Papers*, 5.

[120] *Cal. S. P. Dom.* (1650-1651), 400, 443.

[121] *Cal. S. P. Dom.* (1650-1651), 11.

[122] Aylmer, *The State's Servants*, 273-74.

[123] PRO SP 23/114 PFF 2768 f. 459.

[124] *Stowe MSS.* 189 F. 14 (Thomas Scot's Confession), 73.

[125] *D. N. B.* (John Bradshaw), Vol II., 1088: quoting *Historical MSS. Commission 5th Report*, 328; *Cal. S. P. Dom.* (1649-1650), 221; C. H. Firth (ed.) "Thomas Scot as Intelligencer," *English Historical Review*, Vol. XII (1897), 121; *Milton State Papers*, 50.

[126] Underdown, *Royalist Conspiracy*, 111.

[127] Underdown, *Revel, Riot and Rebellion*, esp. chapters eight and nine.

[128] *Ibid., Royalist Conspiracy*, 20.

[129] *Ibid.*, 1.

[130] *Ibid.*, 44.

[131] *Milton State Papers*, 39.

[132] *D. N. B.*, Vol. I. (William Craven), 45-49.

[133] George Bishop, *A Rejoinder Consisting of Two Parts* (London: Thomas Simmons, 1658), 34-35.

[134] Underdown, *Royalist Conspiracy*, 42-43; Milton State Papers, 49.

[135] Gardiner, *History of Commonwealth and Protectorate*, Vol. I, 193.

[136] *Milton State Papers*, 39; Ibid., Vol. II, 8-9.

[137] Underdown, *Royalist Conspiracy*, 40-45.

[138] *Milton State Papers*, 37.

[139] *Ibid.*, 39.

[140] *Ibid.*, 39.

141 BL E 1071 (2), *The Lord Craven's Case, As to the Confiscation and Sale of His Estate by Judgment of Parliament. Related and Argued, and Objections Answered on the Behalf of the Commonwealth* (London: Printed by William Du Gard, 1653); *Cal. S. P. Dom.* (1652-1653), 102.

142 *Cal. S. P. Dom.* (1651), 69.

143 *Cal. S. P. Dom.* (1651), 74.

144 BL E 1071 (3), *A Reply to a Certain Pamphlet Written by an Unknowing and Unknown Author* (London: R. White, 1653), 2.

145 BL E 1971 (2), *The Lord Craven's Case*, 5; *Cal. S. P. Dom.* (1651-1652), 92, 286.

146 *Ibid.*, 3.

147 BL E 234 (4), *The Lord Craven's Case, Briefly Stated* (London: Thom. Newcomb, 1654), 7.

148 D. H. Sacks, 'The Corporate Town,' 82-83.

149 Martin, 'The Pre-Quaker Writings of George Bishop,' 24-25.

150 George Bishop, *A Rejoinder Consisting of Two Parts*, 32-42.

151 *Ibid.*, 32-35.

152 *Ibid.*, 36-37.

153 *Milton State Papers*, 50.

154 *Ibid.*

155 *Ibid.*, 54.

156 Underdown, *Royalist Conspiracy*, 47-48.

157 G.D. Owen, 'The Conspiracy of Christopher Love,' *The Transactions of the Honourable Society of Cymmrodorions, Session 1966*, 36; Gardiner, *History of Commonwealth and Protectorate* Vol. II., 13; Underdown, *Royalist Conspiracy*, 46-47; Worden, *The Rump Parliament*, 243-44.

158 Owen, 'The Conspiracy of Christopher Love,' 93; *D.N.B.* (Christopher Love) Vol. XII, 55-57.

159 *Ibid.*, Owen, 95.

160 *D.N.B.* (Christopher Love)

161 Worden, *The Rump Parliament*, 247; *D.N.B.* (Love), 155-57.

162 J.W. Willis-Bund, *A Selection of Cases from the State Trials Vol. I. Trials for Treason* (Cambridge: Cambridge University Press, 1879), 623.

163 *Ibid.*, 636; C.H. Firth, 'Thomas Scot as Intelligencer,' 121.

164 *Milton State Papers*, 75.

165 *Ibid.*

166 *Ibid.*

167 Worden, 'Providence and Politics in Cromwellian England,' 99.

168 Bishop, *A Rejoinder Consisting of Two Parts*, 70; *B.L. Stowe MSS.* 189 f. 14 (Thomas Scot's Confession), 72-73.

[169] Martin, 'The Pre-Quaker Writings of George Bishop'; *Milton State Papers*, 75; *A Short Plea for the Commonwealth in this Monstrous and Shaking Juncture* (London, 1651), esp. 14-16.

[170] Ralph Farmer, *Satan Inthron'd* (London: Edw. Thomas, 1657), 115.

[171] Patricia Crawford, 'Charles Stuart, That Man of Blood,' *Journal of British Studies*. 16 (1977) 41.

[172] Bishop, *A Rejoinder*, 79.

[173] *Ibid.*, 81.

[174] *A Short Plea for the Commonwealth*, 15.

[175] Worden, *The Rump Parliament*, 244.

[176] *Ibid.*, 238.

[177] Martin, 'The Pre-Quaker Writings of George Bishop,' 21; Underdown, *Royalist Conspiracy*, 42 ff.

[178] *Cal. S.P. Dom.* (1651) 364-65.

[179] *Cal. S.P. Dom.* (1651-1652) 39; Bodleian Lib., MSS. Tanner LV, 37-39 (Robert Stapylton to Geo. Bishop).

[180] Morrill, *The Revolt of the Provinces*, 181-82, 204.

[181] George Bishop to Edward Winslow, PRO SP 23/114 PFF 2768, 455; *D.N.B.* (Edw. Winslow) Vol. XXI, 672-74.

[182] *Cal. S.P. Dom.* (1651-1652) 285.

[183] George Bishop to Bulstrode Whitelocke, Longleat-Whitelocke Papers, Vol. XII., 167a-168b; Bishop, *A Manifesto Declaring*, 23.

[184] Longleat-Whitelocke Papers, Vol. XII., 170b.

[185] Hirst, *Authority and Conflict*, 309.

[186] Longleat-Whitelocke Papers, Vol. XII., 170a.

[187] Abbott, *The Writings and Speeches of Oliver Cromwell*, Vol. II., 589.

[188] *Ibid.*

[189] *Ibid.*

[190] Bishop, *Warnings*, 12.

[191] Bishop, *Mene Tekel*, 46.

[192] *Ibid.*, 49.

[193] A.H. Woolrych, 'Oliver Cromwell and the Rule of the Saints,' R.H. Parry, *The English Civil War and After 1642-1658*, (Berkeley: University of California Press, 1970).

[194] *Ibid.*, 59-67.

[195] Abbott, *The Writings and Speeches of Oliver Cromwell*, Vol. III., 64-65.

[196] Woolrych, 'Oliver Cromwell and the Rule of the Saints'; Woolrych, *Commonwealth to Protectorate*, esp. Chapter Ten.

[197] George Bishop, *The Throne of Truth Exalted* (London: Giles Calvert, 1657), 104.

[198] In his *Warnings*, Bishop quoted excerpts from Cromwell's 4 July 1653 speech to illustrate how it promised liberty of conscience and the establishment of godly rule, and to point out in retrospect how Cromwell had betrayed that promise.

[199] *Cal. S. P. Dom.* (1653-1654), 14.

[200] *Ibid.*, (1652-1653), 143.

[201] Bishop, *Mene Tekel*, 48; Abbott, *The Writings and Speeches of Oliver Cromwell*, Vol. III 593- 95; Gardiner, *History of Commonwealth and Protectorate*, Vol. II., 200-202.

[202] *Cal. S. P. Dom.* (1653-1654), 133-34.

[203] Longleat-Whitelocke Papers, Vol. XIV, 182.

[204] Sacks, *Widening Gate,* chapter eight.

[205] *Bristol Lists: Municipal and Miscellaneous*, A.B. Beaven (compiler) (Bristol: T.D. Taylor and Sons and Hawkins, 1899), 185, 198-200, 223.

[206] Underdown, *Revel, Riot and Rebellion*, 226.

[207] *Cal. S. P. Dom.* (1654), 321-322.

[208] Cole, 'The Quakers and Politics,' 237.

[209] *Biographical Dictionary of Seventeenth Century Radicals* 'Dennis Hollister' R. L. Graves, Vol. II.

[210] P. G. Rogers, *The Fifth Monarchy Men* (London: Oxford University Press, 1966), 14-17.

[211] Farmer, *Satan Inthron'd*, 46.

[212] *Cal. S. P. Dom.* (1653-1654), 255.

[213] R. Farmer, *The Lord Craven's Case Stated and The Imposter Dethron'd*, (London: Edward Thomas, 1660), 62.

[214] *Cal. S. P. Dom.* (1653-1654), 332.

[215] *Deposition Books of Bristol.* Vol. II. 1650-1654. D. Douglas (ed.) (Bristol: Bristol Record Society, 1948), 6-7.

[216] *Ibid.*, 179.

[217] Sacks, 1991 (272), *Widening Gate.*

[218] *Cal. S. P. Dom.* (1653-1654), 332.

[219] *The Annals of Bristol in the Seventeenth Century*, John Latimer (ed.) (Bristol: William George's Sons, 1900), 251.

[220] *Ibid.*

[221] B. Reay, *Radical Religion*, see Chapter One.

[222] Farmer, *The Great Mysteries*, A.4.

[223] *Ibid.*

[224] For the fullest, most balanced account of Fox's founding and leadership role, see: H. Larry Ingle, *First Among Friends, George and the Creation of Quakerism.* (New York and Oxford: Oxford University Press, 1994).

225 *The Encyclopedia of Religion and Ethics*, J. Hastings (ed.) Vol. III. (New York: Charles Scribner's Sons): citing *The Journal of George Fox*, 1901 edition, 1343.; Braithwaite, *The Beginnings of Quakerism*, Chapter One.

226 Barbour, *The Quakers in Puritan England*, esp. 46; Braithwaite, *The Beginnings of Quakerism*, 99-105, 140-41; M. J. Galgano, 'John Bradshaw,' *Biographical Dictionary of British Radicals in the Seventeenth Century*, Vol. I., 87-89.

227 T. P. O'Malley, 'The Press and Quakerism 1653-1659,' *The Journal of the Friends' Historical Society*, Vol. 54, #4, 1979.

228 Braithwaite, *The Beginnings of Quakerism*; 135-36; R. S. Mortimer, *Early Bristol Quakerism: The Society of Friends in the City 1654-1700* (Bristol: The Historical Association, 1967), 2.

229 Bishop, *The Throne of Truth*, 106; BL E 731 (4) W. Erbury, *Jack Pudding Or a Minister Made a Black-Pudding* (London, 1653), 2.

230 Braithwaite, *The Beginnings of Quakerism*, 165-70.

231 Bishop, *The Throne of Truth*, 106.

232 *A. R. Barclay Manuscript, A Listing Prepared for the Society of Friends*, London, 1976 by C. W. Horle, Vol. I., 182; *The Caton Manuscript. A Listing Prepared for the Society of Friends*, London, by C. W Horle, Vol. III., 061-063; (For the manuscripts that were edited by Horle, I have modernized the spelling and punctuation. The brackets are Horle's. Horle, 'John Camm: Profile of a Quaker Minister during the Interregnum,' *Quaker History*, 70 (1981), 78-81.

233 R. S. Mortimer, 'Bristol Quaker Merchants: Some New Seventeenth-Century Evidence,' *The Journal of the Friends' Historical Society*, Vol. 45, Number 2. (Autumn 1953): 8; R. T. Vann, *The Social Development of Quakerism 1655-1755* (Cambridge, Ma.: Harvard University Press, 1969) esp. Chapter II.

234 *The Records of a Church of Christ in Bristol, 1640-1687*, R. Hayden (ed.) (Bristol: Bristol Record Society, 1974), 106.

235 Bishop, *The Salutation of Love to the Seed of God in the People Called Independents, Baptists, Monarchy-Men and Seekers*, (London: Robert Wilson, 1661) 7; Capp, *The Fifth Monarchy Men*, 57-58, 64-66.

236 M. J. Galgano, 'John Bradshaw,' *Biographical Dictionary of Seventeenth-Century British Radicals*, Vol. I., 87-87.

237 *A. R. Barclay Manuscript*, Vol. I., 182.

238 Bishop, et al., *The Cry of Blood and Herod*, (London: Giles Calvert, 1656), 1.

239 W. James, *The Varieties of Religious Experience: A Study in Human Nature, Being the Gifford Lectures on Natural Religion Delivered at Edinburgh University in 1901-1902* (New York: New American Library, 1958) esp. Lectures VIII-X.

240 Bishop, *Jesus Christ the Same*, 4.

241 Beaven, *Bristol Lists: Municipal and Miscellaneous*.

242 Bishop, *Warnings*, 6.

243 *The Constitutional Documents of the Puritan Revolution 1625-1660*, S.R. Gardiner (ed.) (Oxford: Oxford University Press, 1906), 416.

244 Bishop, *The Cry of Blood*, 5-6.

245 *Ibid.*

246 L. Strauss, *Persecution and the Art of Writing*, (Glencoe, Ill: The Free Press Publishers, 1952), 33-34.

247 Friends House Library, London, *The Great Books of Sufferings*, Vol. I., 81.

248 Bishop, *Jesus Christ the Same*, 4-17.

249 *Ibid.* 22.

250 *Ibid.* 25.

251 *Ibid.* 21-28. In the works he wrote after the 1662 Quaker Act, Bishop drew the distinction between the worldly and spiritual realms by analyzing their metaphysical natures.

252 Bishop, *The Cry of Blood*, 137.

253 Public Record Office, London, Eng., RG 6/666, *Society of Friends Book Number 123, Monthly Meeting of the Society of Friends in Bristol in Somersetshire, Burials, 1655-1779*, 1.

254 Bishop, *The Cry of Blood*, 19.

255 R.S. Mortimer, 'Quakerism in Seventeenth-Century Bristol' (unpublished M.A. thesis), Univ. of Bristol, 1946, 6-7.

256 Bishop, *Jesus Christ the Same*, 26.

257 Bishop, *The Throne of Truth*, 55.

258 Bishop, *The Cry of Blood*, 27-28; Braithwaite, *The Beginnings of Quakerism*, 171-72.

259 *Ibid. The Cry of Blood*, 29.

260 *Ibid.*, 29, 31; *The Throne of Truth*, 56.

261 B. Reay, 'Popular Hostility Towards Quakers in Mid-Seventeenth-Century England,' *Social History*, number 5, (October 1980): 403-04.

262 Bishop, *The Cry of Blood*, 35.

263 Latimer, *The Annals of Bristol in the Seventeenth Century*, 257; R.S. Mortimer, *Quakerism in Seventeenth Century Bristol*, 10.

264 *Ibid.* Mortimer, 11.

265 G. Fox, *The Journal of George Fox*, R. Jones (ed.) (New York: Capricorn Books, 1963), 223.

266 *Barclay MSS*, 205-06.

267 Woolrych, *Penruddock's Rising*, 3.

268 Bodleian Library, *Rawlinson MSS. A. 23. f. 213*. George Bishop to John Thurloe, 21 February 1655.

269 Underdown, *Royalist Conspiracy*, 135; Latimer, *The Annals of Bristol in the Seventeenth Century*, 20.

270 *Rawlinson MSS*, A. 23. f. 145. George Bishop to John Thurloe, 17 February 1655.

271 *Ibid.*

272 *Ibid.*, 97.

273 *Thurloe State Papers*, Vol. III., 172.

274 *Thurloe State Papers*, Vol. III, 177.

275 *Ibid.*

276 *Ibid.*, 177.

277 *Thurloe State Papers*, Vol. III., 171.

278 *Ibid.*, 171-72, 177.

279 *Ibid.*, 172.

280 *Ibid.*

281 C.H. Firth *Oliver Cromwell's Army: A History of the English Soldier During the Civil Wars, the Commonwealth and the Protectorate*, (London: Methuen and Company Ltd., 1911), 366-68. B. Taft, 'The Humble Petition of Several Colonels of the Army: Causes, Character, and Results of Military Opposition to Cromwell's Protectorate, *Huntington Library Quarterly*, Vol. 42 Number 1 (Winter 1978); *Thurloe State Papers*, Vol. III., 147-48.

282 Raab, *The English Face of Machiavelli*, 130-50.

283 Gardiner, *History of the Commonwealth and Protectorate*, Vol. III., 21.

284 The punishment of the three officers who initiated the petition served to illustrate their grievance. Firth tells us: 'Col. Alured was cashiered, Col. Okey was allowed to resign, Col. Saunders ... retained his command for a time, but lost his commission later.' Firth, *Cromwell's Army*, 367 and note 1.

285 Underdown, *Royalist Conspiracy*, 27-58; Woolrych, *Penruddock's Rising*, 17-19.

286 *Thurloe State Papers*, Vol. III., 242.

287 *Ibid.*, 268 Birch printed Farmer's name as Harmer, a spelling that sometimes appeared in contemporary documents.

288 *Rawlinson MSS.*, A. 24 f. 295-96, George Bishop to John Thurloe 26 February 1655.

289 *Ibid.*

290 *Ibid. Rawlinson MSS.* A. 26. f. 296, George Bishop to John Thurloe 22 May 1655.

291 *Ibid.*

292 Reay, *The Quakers and the English Revolution*, 11.

293 *Extracts from State Papers Relating to Friends 1654-1672*, N. Penney (ed.) (London: Headley Bros., 1913), 1.

294 The use of silence in Quaker meetings is fully explored in R. Bauman, *Let Your Words Be Few: Symbolism of Speaking and Silence among Seventeenth-Century Quakers*, (Cambridge: Cambridge University Press, 1989)

295 *Ibid.*, see esp. 84-92.

[296] *Ibid.*, 87.

[297] *Ibid.*, 89. For a full discussion on the prophesying of the radical sectaries see Hill, *The World Turned Upside Down*, Chapter Six.

[298] Bishop, *Warnings*, 14.

[299] K. Thomas, *Religion and the Decline of Magic*, (New York: Charles Scribner's Sons, 1971) esp. Chapters 16 and 17.

[300] *Ibid.*, 487; Reay, *The Quakers and The English Revolution*, 68-71.

[301] *The Devil Turned Quaker*, (London: Printed for John Andrews, 1656), A.6.

[302] Thomas, *Religion and the Decline of Magic*, 487.

[303] Bishop, *Warnings*, 5.

[304] B. Worden, 'Toleration and The Cromwellian Protectorate,' *Persecution and Toleration: Papers Read at the Twenty Second Summer Meeting and the Twenty-Third Winter Meeting of the Ecclesiastical History Society*, W. J. Shiels (ed.) (London: Basil Blackwell, 1984)

[305] Abbott, *The Writings and Speeches of Oliver Cromwell*, Vol. III., 627.

[306] Bishop, *The Cry of Blood*, 112.

[307] Ibid., *The Cry of Blood*, 123-25.

[308] Fox, et al. *The West Answering to the North* (London: Giles Calvert, 1656) Although Bishop is not credited as a co-author in sources like Smith, Wing, or Fortescue; Braithwaite found that Fox named Bishop as the author of the tract in an unpublished history of Quakerism. See Braithwaite, *The Beginnings of Quakerism*, 562. H. J. Cadbury also noted this information in 'The Swarthmore Documents in America,' *The Journal of Friends' Historical Society*, Supplement No. 20, 1940, 24. I thank Dr. J. W. Martin for bringing this essential point to my attention. In addition, I have found that various letters in *The Original Record of Sufferings*, edited by C. W. Horle, confirms that Bishop wrote a major portion of the tract, edited the entire work, and guided it through publication.

[309] *Ibid.*, 1.

[310] Barbour, *The Quakers in Puritan England*, 62; Bishop, *The Throne of Truth*, 105; Braithwaite, *The Beginnings of Quakerism*, 232-34; Fox, *The West Answering to the North*, 10.

[311] For a fuller discussion of this aspect of Bishop's work in 1656, see Maryann Feola, '"Warringe with Ye Worlde": Fox's Relationship with Nayler,' *Quaker History*, 81 No. 2 (Fall 1992), 63-72; rpt. in *New Light on George Fox 1624-1691: A Collection of Essays*, M. Mullett ed. York, Eng. *Sessions of York, The Ebor Press*, 1994.

[312] *Original Record of Sufferings*, No. 299, 095.

[313] *Ibid.*, No. 305, 102-03, and No. 610, 224-25.

[314] *Ibid.*, No. 622, 235.

[315] *Ibid.*

[316] *Ibid.*, No. 610, 224.

[317] *Ibid.*, esp. Nos. 298-300, 091-096.

[318] Fox, *The West Answering to the North*, 4.

[319] *Ibid.*, 1-16.

[320] *Ibid.*, 28, 16-31; *Original Record of Sufferings*, 097-098.

[321] Bishop, *Warnings*, 11.

[322] *Ibid.*, 8.

[323] *Ibid.*, 8-9.

[324] *Ibid.*, 10; Mortimer, 'Quakerism in Seventeenth-Century Bristol,' 337 and note 2.

[325] *Original Record of Sufferings*, No. 305, 102.

[326] Cadbury, 'The Swarthmore Documents in America,' 24.

[327] *Ibid.*, 25.

[328] *Ibid.*

[329] Braithwaite, *The Beginnings of Quakerism*, 388.

[330] Quoted in: Braithwaite, *The Beginning of Quakerism*, 388. Braithwaite found that in this quote 'strength' should be corrected as 'string,' as it is a reference to the common accusation that the Quakers put strings and ribbons on the arms of people they bewitched. 574.

[331] P. Mack, 'Women as Prophets during the English Civil War,' *The Origins of Anglo-American Radicalism*, J. R. Jacob and M. C. Jacob eds. (London: George Allen & Unwin, 1984): 222-25; also see Mack's *Visionary Women: Escstatic Prophecy in Seventeenth-Century England*, (Berkeley, University of California Press) 1989, esp. chapter two.

[332] Braithwaite, *The Beginning of Quakerism*, 389.

[333] Bishop, *The Throne of Truth*, 52-53.

[334] *Ibid.*, 4, Braithwaite, *The Beginnings of Quakerism*, 247.

[335] W. G. Bittle, *James Nayler 1618-1660: The Quaker Indicted by Parliament* (Richmond, Indiana, Friends United Press and Sessions of York, England, 1986), 84.

[336] Bishop, *The Throne of Truth*, 20.

[337] *Ibid.*, 4-5.

[338] Friends House Library, London, *Letters and Documents of Early Friends*. Vol. I., No. 188, 221. George Bishop to Margaret Fell, 27 October 1656.

[339] S. W. Angell 'The Rise of Elderism within Quakerism,' *Friends Consultation on Eldering Conference Proceedings*, (Richmond, Indiana, Quaker Hill Conference Center, 1982), 1.

[340] D. J. Hall 'An Historical Study of the Discipline of the Society of Friends 1738-1861,' Unpublished Thesis for the Degree of Master of Arts Durham University, 1972, 180.

[341] R. Lockyer and J. Mason (eds.), *James Nayler and the Protectorate*, (York, Eng.: Longman Group Ltd., 1980) 5.

[342] Bishop, *The Throne of Truth*, 3.

[343] Bittle, *James Nayler*, 86.

[344] Bishop, *The Throne of Truth*, 4.

[345] Mack, 'Women as Prophets during the English Civil War,' 221-22 and her note number 42; for an in-depth discussion of Simmonds' influence on Nayler, see Mack, *Visionary Women*, 197-208.

[346] Bishop, *The Throne of Truth*, 4.

[347] *Original Record of Sufferings*, No. 622, 235-36.

[348] *Ibid.*

[349] *Ibid.*, No. 286, 80.

[350] *Ibid.*

[351] *Letters and Documents of Early Friends*, Vol. I., No. 188, 221.

[352] Lockyer and Mason, *Nayler*, 5.

[353] Bishop, *The Throne of Truth*, 4.

[354] *Ibid.*, 9.

[355] *Letters and Documents of Early Friends*, Vol. Il, No. 188, 221-22.

[356] *Ibid.*, 222.

[357] *Ibid.*, 223.

[358] Worden, 'Toleration and the Cromwellian Protectorate,' 225.

[359] *The Devil Turned Quaker*, A.3.

[360] *Ibid.*, A.4.

[361] Mack, 'Women as Prophets during the English Civil War,' 222.

[362] *The Devil Turned Quaker*, A.6.

[363] *Letters and Documents of Early Friends*, Vol. I, No. 188, 221.

[364] Bittle, *James Nayler*, 110.

[365] *Ibid.*, 110-11. He mistakenly footnoted Farmer's *Satan Inthron'd*, 34-36. The information is found instead in Grigge's *The Quakers' Jesus*, 34-36.

[366] *Ibid.*

[367] I*bid.*

[368] J. T. Rutt (ed.), *The Diary of Thomas Burton, Esq., Member in the Parliaments of Oliver and Richard Cromwell from 1656 to 1659* (London: Henry Colburn, 1828), Vol. I., 10.

[369] Worden, 'Toleration and the Cromwellian Protectorate,' 218-19.

[370] *Ibid.*, 207-09; W. K. Jordan *The History of Religious Toleration in England*, Vol. I., 17.

[371] *Ibid.* Worden, 218.

[372] *Ibid.*, 203; For a full discussion of the contemporary fear of Socinianism see H. J. McLachlan, *Socinianism in Seventeenth-Century England*, Oxford: Oxford University Press, 1951.

[373] Rutt, *The Diary of Thomas Burton*, Vol. I., 48-50.

[374] Bishop, *The Throne of Truth*, 96-97.

[375] Bishop, *A Rejoinder Consisting of Two Parts*, 177-78.

[376] Rutt, *The Diary of Thomas Burton*, Vol. I., 96-167.

[377] Abbott, *The Writings and Speeches of Oliver Cromwell*, Vol. IV., 336.

[378] See especially Bittle, *James Nayler*, Chapters IV and V; Hill, *The Experience of Defeat*, 129, 138-42; Hirst, *Conflict and Authority*, 342-48; Reay, *The Quakers and the English Revolution*, 53-55; Worden, 'Toleration and the Cromwellian Protectorate,' 220-26.

[379] *Quarterly Meeting of Bristol and Somersetshire Burials 1651-1837*, 1, 2.

[380] *A.R. Barclay MSS*, Vol. I., No. 13, 18-20.

[381] Farmer, *Satan Inthron'd*, A3-A4.

[382] *Ibid.*, 35-40.

[383] Bishop, *The Throne of Truth*, 18-19.

[384] *Ibid.*, 3-7, 20.

[385] *Ibid.*

[386] Gardiner, *The Constitutional Documents of the Puritan Revolution*, 455.

[387] *Ibid.*, 454.

[388] *Ibid.*

[389] McLachlan, *Socinianism in Seventeenth Century England*, 1-23.

[390] Worden, 'Toleration and the Cromwellian Protectorate,' 220.

[391] Bittle, *James Nayler*, 122.

[392] Bishop, *The Throne of Truth*, 20.

[393] *Ibid.*, 67-71.

[394] *Ibid.*, 70.

[395] *Ibid.*, 63.

[396] Reay, *The Quakers and the English Revolution*, 56-57.

[397] *Ibid.*, see especially Chapter 4.

[398] Penney, *State Papers Relating to Friends*, 37-61.

[399] *Ibid.*, 50, 52.

[400] *Ibid.*, 39.

[401] Firth and Rait, *Acts and Ordinances of the Interregnum*, Vol. II., 1098-1100, 1162-70; Reay, *Radical Religion in the English Revolution*, 159-60.

[402] Abbott, *The Writings and Speeches of Oliver Cromwell*, Vol. IV., 545-46; Rutt, *The Diary of Thomas Burton*, Vol. I., 376, Vol. II., 202-03.

[403] Worden, 'Toleration and the Cromwellian Protectorate,' 297.

[404] G. Davies, *The Restoration of Charles II, 1658-1660* (San Marino, Ca.; Huntington Library, 1955), 28.

[405] In particular see Bishop's *Warnings of the Lord* and his *Mene Tekel*.

[406] Bishop, *Warnings*, 17.

407 Davies, *The Restoration of Charles II*, 27.

408 *Ibid.*

409 Bishop, *Warnings*, 17.

410 Davies, *The Restoration of Charles II*, 27-28.

411 Cole, 'The Quakers and Politics,' 326.

412 Firth, *Cromwell's Army*, 371-74; A.H. Woolrych, 'The Good Old Cause and the Fall of the Protectorate,' *Cambridge Historical Journal*, Vol. XIII, No. I (1957): 133-61.

413 Quoted in: J.F. Maclear 'Quakerism and the End of the Interregnum': A Chapter in Domestication of Radical Puritanism,' *Church History*, XIX (December 1950: 259.

414 Cole 'The Quakers and Politics,' 90.

415 Maclear, 'Quakerism and the End of the Interregnum,' 259.

416 Cole, 'The Quakers and Politics,' 85.

417 Bishop, *Warnings*. 19.

418 *Ibid.*

419 *Ibid.*

420 Bishop, *Mene Tekel*, 9.

421 *Ibid.*, 10.

422 *Ibid.*, 19.

423 Cole, 'The Quakers and Politics,' 92.

424 Bishop, *Warnings*, 23-26.

425 Bishop, *Mene Tekel*, 48.

426 A.W. Braithwaite, 'Early Tithe Prosecutions: Friends as Outlaws,' *The Journal of Friends' Historical Society* 49, No. 3 (1960): 148-56.

427 Bishop, *Warnings*, 25.

428 A. Cole, 'The Quakers and the English Revolution,' *Past and Present*, No. 10 (November 1956): 46; Maclear, *Quakerism and the End of the Interregnum*, 255-56.

429 Bishop, *Warnings*, 35; Reay, *The Quakers and the English Revolution*, 85.

430 Bishop, *Warnings*, 35; Cole, *The Quakers and Politics*, 104.

431 BL E 983 (7) *The Humble Petition and Address of the Officers of the Army to the Parliament of the Commonwealth* (London: H. Hills and F. Tyton, 1659) 7.

432 *Ibid.*

433 Bishop, *Mene Tekel*, 28.

434 *Ibid.*, 38-39.

435 *Ibid.*, 27.

436 *Ibid.*, Al.

437 Davies, *The Restoration of Charles II*, 144.

[438] A.H. Woolrych, 'Milton and Cromwell: 'A Short but Scandalous Night of Interruption',' in *The Achievements of the Left Hand: Essays on the Prose of John Milton.* (M. Lieb and J.T. Shawcross (eds.) (Amherst: University of Massachusetts Press, 1974) 258.

[439] Quoted in: Davies, *The Restoration of Charles II*, 108.

[440] Davies, *The Restoration of Charles II*, 147-48.

[441] Quoted in: Reay, *The Quakers and the English Revolution*, 87.

[442] F. D. Dow *Radicalism in the English Revolution, 1645-1660* (Oxford and New York: Basil Blackwell, 1985) 73.

[443] Braithwaite, *The Beginnings of Quakerism*, 462.

[444] Reay, *The Quakers and the English Revolution*, 85-86.

[445] Bishop, *Warnings*, 35.

[446] *Ibid.*

[447] *Ibid.*, 34-47; Cole, 'The Quakers and Politics, 178.

[448] Bishop, *Ibid.*, 24.

[449] *Ibid.*, 34-35.

[450] Maclear, 'Quakerism and the End of the Interregnum,' 267.

[451] Bishop, *Mene Tekel* and *Warnings*.

[452] Seyers, Samuel, *Memoirs Historical and Topographical of Bristol and Its Neighborhood* (Bristol: John Gutch, 1821) Vol. I., 507-08.

[453] Mortimer, 'Quakerism in Seventeenth Century Bristol,' 22-23.

[454] *Ibid.*, 23.

[455] Mortimer, 'Quakerism in Seventeenth Century Bristol,' 22.

[456] R. Greaves, *Deliver Us From Evil: The Radical Underground in Britain, 1660-1663* (New York: Oxford University Press, 1986), 3.

[457] Bishop, *Warnings*, 42.

[458] Bishop, *To Thee Charles Stuart*, 6.

[459] Greaves, *Deliver Us From Evil*, 48.

[460] Jonathan Barry, 'The Politics of Religion in Restoration Bristol,' *The Politics of Religion in Restoration England*, T. Harris, P. Seaward and M. Goldie eds. (Oxford: Basil Blackwell Ltd., 1990): 165.

[461] Joseph Besse, *A Collection of Sufferings of the People Called Quakers.* 2 Vols. (London: Luke Hinde, 1753). I, 42.

[462] Nathaniel Hawthorne, *The Scarlet Letter.* Case Studies in Contemporary Criticism, ed. R.C. Murfin (Boston: Bedford Books of St. Martin's Press, 1991).

[463] George Bishop, *An Illumination to Open the Eyes of Papists.* (London 1661, 1662): 10.

BIBLIOGRAPHY

MANUSCRIPTS

Bodleian Library, Oxford
        Rawlinson MS
        Tanner MS

Bristol Record Office
        Ale House Licence Book, 05062/1
        The Burgess Book 1607-1659
        Sessions Books
        Supplement of the Quarterly Meeting of Bristol and
            Somersetshire, Births 1653-1784.
        Quarterly Meeting of Bristol and Somersetshire Burials,
            1651-1677.

British Library
        Additional MS 403 Naval Papers 1643-1677
        Stowe MS 189
        Stowe MS 575 Historical Letters and Papers 1641-1660

Friends Historical Library, Swarthmore College
        Penn MS

Friends House Library, London
        A R Barclay MS, A Listing Prepared by C.W. Horle
        Caton MS, A Listing Prepared by C.W. Horle
        Dictionary of Quaker Biography
        Etting MS
        Letters and Documents of Early Friends Vol. I.
        The Original Record of Sufferings, Vols. V-VIII, Compiled
            by C.W. Horle

Institute of Historical Research, University of London
        Longleat-Whitelocke Papers

Public Record Office, London
Probated Wills
Society of Friends Book Number 123, Monthly Meeting of
the Society of Friends in Bristol and Somersetshire,
Burials, 1655-1779
State Papers Domestic

Taunton Record Office
Dickinson MS DD/DN 199

PRINTED SOURCES

A Declaration and Ordinance of the Lords and Commons Assembled in Parliament for Seizing and Sequestering. London: Edward Husbands, 1643.

A Reply to a Certain Pamphlet Written by an Unknowing and Unknown Author. London: R. White, 1653.

A Short Plea for the Commonwealth in this Monstrous and Shaking Juncture. London, 1651.

Besse, Joseph *A Collection of the Sufferings of the People Called Quakers*. London: Luke Hinde, 1752.

A True Relation of the Storming of Bristol and the Taking of the Town, Castle, Forts, Ordinances, Ammunition and Arms by Sir Thomas Fairfax's Army London: Printed for Edward Husbands, 1645.

Beaven, Alfred B. *Bristol Lists: Municipal and Miscellaneous*. Bristol: T.D. Taylor, Sons and Hawkins, 1899.

Besse, Joseph. *A Collection of Sufferings of the People Called Quakers*. 2 vols. London: Luke Hinde, 1753.

Birch, Thomas *Collection of the State Papers of John Thurloe, Esq. Secretary, First to the Council of State, and Afterwards to the Two Protectors, Oliver and Richard Cromwell*. 7 vols. London: Charles Davis, 1742.

Bishop, George. *A More Particular and Exact Relation of the Victory*. London: R. Cotes, 1645.

——— *A Modest Check to Part of a Scandalous Libel*. London: c.1650.

——— *Jesus Christ, The Same Today*. London: Giles Calvert, 1655.

——— et al. *The Cry of Blood and Herod*, London: Giles Calvert, 1656.

——— *The Throne of Truth*. London: Giles Calvert, 1657.

——— *A Rejoinder Consisting of Two Parts* London: Thomas Simmons, 1658.

—— *Mene Tekel* London: Thomas Brewster, 1659.

—— *The Warnings of the Lord*. London: M. Inman and Bristol: R. Moon, 1660.

—— *A Tender Visitation to Both Universities* London: R. Wilson, Bristol: R. Moon, 1660.

—— *To Thee Charles Stuart King of England*. Bristol: 1660.

—— *The Salutation of Love to the Seed of God in the People Called Independents, Baptists, Monarchy-Men and Seekers*. London: Robert Wilson, 1661.

—— *An Illumination to Open the Eyes of Papists*. London: 1661, 1662.

—— *A Little Treatise Concerning Sufferings*. London: 1663.

—— *A Manifesto Declaring*, 1665.

—— *A Looking-Glass for the Times*, London: 1668.

Burton, Henry. *A Vindication of Churches Commonly Called Independent* London: Printed for Henry Overton, 1644.

Carlisle, Nicholas. *A Concise Dictionary of the Endowed Grammar Schools in England and Wales* London: Baldwin and Cardock and Joy, 1818.

Erbury, W. *Jack Pudding Or a Minister Made a Black-Pudding* London, 1653.

Farmer, Ralph *Satan Inthron'd* London: Edward Thomas, 1657.

—— *The Great Mysteries of Godlinesse and Ungodlinesse*. London and Bristol: J. Kirton and W. Ballard, 1654.

—— *The Lord Craven's Case Stated and The Imposter Dethron'd*. London: Edward Thomas, 1660.

Firth, C.H. ed. *The Clarke Papers. Selections from the Papers of William Clarke, Secretary to the Council of the Army, 1647-1649, and to General Monck and the Commanders of the Army in Scotland, 1651-1660*. 4 vols. London: Printed for the Camden Society, 1891.

—— ed. *The Memoirs of Edmund Ludlow Lieutenant-General of the Horse in the Army of the Commonwealth of England 1625-1672* Vol. I. Oxford: The Clarendon Press, 1894.

Forster, Joseph *Alumni Oxonienses: The Members of the University of Oxford 1500-1714, Their Parentage, Birthplace and Year of Birth, With a Record of Their Degrees Being the Matriculated Register of the University*. Oxford: Parker and Company, 1888.

Fox, George. et al. *The West Answering to the North*. London: Giles Calvert, 1656.

Greene, Mary Anne E. *Calendar of State Papers, Domestic Series*. London: Her Majesty's Stationery Office 1858-93.

—— *Calendar of the Proceedings of the Committee for Compounding 1643-1660*. London: Her Majesty's Stationery Office, 1892.

Hollister, Dennis *The Skirts of the Whore Discovered* London: Giles Calvert, 1656.

Latimer, John ed. *The Annals of Bristol in the Seventeenth Century*. Bristol: William George's Sons, 1900.

Lt. General Oliver Cromwell's Letter to the House of Commons of All the Particulars of the Taking of the City of Bristol. London: Edward Husbands, 1648.

Nickolls, J. ed. *Original Letters and Papers of State Addressed to Oliver Cromwell Concerning the Affairs of Great Britain from the Year 1649-1658, Found among the Political Collections of John Milton*. London: William Boyer, 1743.

Phillimore, W.P.W. *Index Nominum to the Royalist Composition Papers*. London: Charles J. Clark, 1889.

Rutt, John T. *Diary of Thomas Burton, Esq. Member in the Parliaments of Oliver and Richard Cromwell, from 1656 to 1659*. London: Henry Colburn, 1828.

Saltmarsh, John. *A Letter from the Army Concerning the Peaceable Temper of the Same*. London: Giles Calvert, 1647.

—— *England's Friend Raised from the Grave*. London: Giles Calvert, 1649.

Sewel, William. *The History of the Rise, Increase and Progress of the Christian People Called Quakers*. Philadelphia: Samuel Keimer, 1728.

Seyer, Samuel. *Memoris Historical and Topographical of Bristol and Its Neighborhood*. Bristol: John Gutch, 1821.

Smith, Joseph. *A Descriptive Catalogue of Friends' Books*. London: Joseph Smith, 1867.

—— *Two Petitions of Divers Free-men of England*. London: Giles Calvert, 1647

Stephen L. and S. Lee eds. *Dictionary of National Biography*. Oxford: Oxford University Press, 1882.

Tanner, William *Three Lectures on the Early History of the Society of Friends in Bristol and Somersetshire*. Phila.: Henry Longstretch, 1858.

The Devil Turned Quaker London: John Andrews, 1656.

The Humble Desires and Proposals of the Private Agitators of Colonel Hewson's Regiment. London: Printed by I.C., 1647.

The Humble Petition and Address of the Officers of the Army to the Parliament of the Commonwealth. London: H. Hills and F. Tyton, 1659.

The Lord Craven's Case, As to the Confiscation and Sale of His Estate by Judgment of Parliament. London: Printed by William Du Gard, 1653.

The Lord Craven's Case, Briefly Stated. London: Thomas Newcomb, 1654.

Willis-Bund, J.W. *A Selection of Cases from the State Trials, Trials for Treason, 1327-1660*. Vol. I. Cambridge: Cambridge University Press, 1879.

PRINTED SECONDARY SOURCES

Abbott, Wilbur C. *The Writing and Speeches of Oliver Cromwell*. 4 Vols. Cambridge: Harvard University Press, 1945.

Agnell, S.W. *Friends Consulation on Eldering Conference Proceedings*. Richmond, Indiana: Quaker Hill Conference Center, 1982.

Aylmer, G.E. *The State's Servants: The Civil Service of the English Republic 1649-1660*. London and Boston: Routledge and Kegal Paul. 1973.

Barbour, Hugh *The Quakers in Puritan England*. New Haven: Yale University Press, 1964.

—— *Early Quaker Writings*. Grand Rapids, Mich.: Eerdmans, 1973.

Bauman, Richard *Let Your Words Be Few: Symbolism of Speaking and Silence among Seventeenth-Century Quakers*. Cambridge: Cambridge University Press, 1983.

Bittle, William G. *James Nayler 1618-1660: The Quaker Indicted by Parliament*. Richmond, Indiana: Friends United Press and Sessions of York, England, 1986.

Braithwaite, Alfred W. 'Early Tithe Prosecutions: Friends as Outlaws,' *The Journal of Friends' Historical Society*. 49 No. 3 (1960): 148-56.

Braithwaite, W. C. *The Beginnings of Quakerism*. Cambridge: Cambridge University Press, 1961 ed.

—— *The Second Period of Quakerism*. Cambridge: Cambridge University Press, 1961 ed.

Cadbury, H.J. 'The Swarthmore Documents in America,' *The Journal of Friends' Historical Society* Supplement No. 20 (1940).

Capp, B.S. *The Fifth Monarchy Men: A Study in Seventeenth-Century English Millenarianism*. Totowa, N.J.: Rowman and Littlefield, 1972.

Cherry, Charles L. 'Enthusiasm and Madness: Anti-Quakerism in the Seventeenth Century,' *Quaker History*. 74 (Fall 1984): 1-24.

Cole, Alan 'The Social Origins of the Early Quakers,' *The Journal of the Friends' Historical Society*. 48 No. 3 (Spring 1957): 99-118.

Crawford, Patricia. 'Charles Stuart, That Man of Blood,' *Journal of British Studies* 16 (1977): 41-69.

Davies, G. *The Restoration of Charles II*. San Marino, Ca.: Huntington Library Press, 1955.

Douglas, D. ed. *Deposition Books of Bristol* Bristol: Bristol Record Society, 1948.

Dow, F.D. *Radicalism in the English Revolution 1640-1660*. Oxford and New York: Basil Blackwell, 1985.

Endy, Melvin B. Jr. 'The Interpretation of Quakerism: Rufus Jones and His Critics.' *Quaker History* 70 (1981): 3-21.

Feola, Maryann S. "'Warringe with Ye World': Fox's Relationship with Nayler,' *Quaker History,* 81 No. 2 (Fall 1992): 63-72. rpt. in *New Light on George Fox 1624-1691: A Collection of Essays.* M. Mullet ed., York, England. Sessions of York/The Ebor Press, 1994.

Firth, C.H. and R.S. Rait *Acts and Ordinances of the Interregnum 1642-1660.* 3 Vols. Holmes Beach, Fla.: Wm. W. Gaunt and Sons, Inc., 1972.

Firth, C.H. *Cromwell's Army: A Study of the English Soldier during the Civil Wars, the Commonwealth and the Protectorate.* London and New York: Methuen and Co. Ltd. and Barnes and Noble, 1911.

—— *The Last Years of the Commonwealth* 2 vols. London: Longmans, Green and Co., 1909.

Foster, Stephen 'The Presbyterian Independents: A Ghost Story for Historians,' *Past and Present,* 44 (1969): 52-75.

—— 'Thomas Scot as Intelligencer,' *English Historical Review.* XII no. 45 (January 1897):116-26.

Fox, George. *The Journal of George Fox, Edited from the Manuscript.* Cambridge: Cambridge University Press, 1911.

—— *The Journal of George Fox.* R. Jones ed. New York: Capricorn Books, 1963.

Fox, J. Charles. *The Royal Forests of England.* London: Methuen and Co., 1905.

Gardiner, Samuel R. *History of the Great Civil War, The Commonwealth and Protectorate 1642-1656.* 4 vols. London: Longmans, Green and Co., 1901.

—— *The Constitutional Documents of the Puritan Revolution 1625-1660* Oxford: Oxford University Press, 1906.

Greaves, R. and R. Zaller eds. *Biographical Dictionary of British Radicals in the Seventeenth Century.* 3 vols. Sussex, Eng.: The Harvester Press, 1982.

Greaves, R. *Deliver Us From Evil: The Radical Underground in Britain, 1660-1663.* New York: Oxford University, 1986.

Harris, Tim, Paul Seward, and Mark Goldie, eds., *The Politics of Religion in Restoration England.* Oxford: Basil Blackwell, 1990.

Hastings, James. *Encyclopedia of Religion and Ethics.* New York: Charles Scribner's Sons, 1951.

Hawthorne, Nathaniel. *The Scarlet Letter.* Case Studies in Contemporary Criticism. ed. R.C. Murfin. Boston: Bedford Books of St. Martin's Press, 1991.

Hayden, R. ed. *The Records of a Church of Christ in Bristol, 1640-1687.* Bristol: Bristol Record Society, 1974.

Hexter, J.H. 'The Problem of the Presbyterian Independents,' *American Historical Review,* xliv (1938-39): 29-49.

Hill, Christopher. *The Century of Revolution 1603-1714.* Edinburgh: T. Nelson, 1961.

—— *The Experience of Defeat: Milton and Some Contemporaries.* New York: Penguin Books, 1984.

—— ed. *The Good Old Cause: The English Revolution of 1640-1660, Its Causes, Course and Consequences.* New York: A.M. Kelley, 1969.

—— *Milton and the English Revolution.* New York: Viking Press, 1978.

—— *The World Turned Upside Down: Radical Ideas during the Puritan Revolution.* Middlesex, Eng.: Penguin Books, 1984.

Hirst, Derek. *Authority and Conflict in England 1603-1658.* London: Edward Arnold Publishers, 1986.

Horle, C.W. 'John Camm: Profile of a Quaker Minister during the Interregnum,' *Quaker History,* 70 (1981).

—— 'Death of a Felon: Richard Vickris and the Elizabethan Conventicle Act.' *Quaker History,* 72, 2 (1987) 95-107.

Ingle, H. Larry. *First Among Friends: George Fox and the Creation of Quakerism.* New York and Oxford: Oxford University Press, 1994.

Jacob, James R. and Margaret C. Jacob., eds., *The Origins of Anglo-American Radicalism.* London: George Allen and Unwin, 1984.

James, William. *The Varieties of Religious Experience: A Study in Human Nature, Being the Gifford Lectures on Natural Religion Delivered at Edinburgh in 1901-1902.* New York: New American Library, 1958.

Jordan, W.K. *Men of Substance: A Study of the Thought of Two English Revolutionaries.* New York: Octagon Books, 1967.

—— *The Development of Religious Toleration in England* 4 vols., Cambridge: Harvard University Press, 1932-1940.

Kaplan, Lawrence, 'Presbyterians and Independents in 1643,' *English Historical Review,* 84, (1969): 244-56.

Kishlansky, Mark, 'The Army and the Levellers: The Roads to Putney' *Historical Journal* XXII, 1979.

—— 'The Case of the Army Stated: The Creation of the New Model Army,' *Past and Present,* No. 81, (1978).

Lamont, William M. *Godly Rule: Politics and Religion 1603-60.* London: MacMillan and Co. Ltd., 1969.

Leib, Michael and John T. Shawcross, eds., *Achievements of the Left Hand: Essays on the Prose of John Milton.* Amherst: The University of Massachusetts Press, 1974.

Lockyer, R. and J. Mason. *James Nayler and the Protectorate Parliament.* York: Longman Group Ltd., 1980.

Mack, Phyllis. *Visionary Women: Ecstatic Prophecy in Seventeenth-Century England.* Berkeley: University of California Press, 1992.

Maclear, J.F. 'Quakerism and the End of the Interregnum: A Chapter in Domestication of Radical Puritanism,' *Church History.* XIX (December 1950): 245-69.

Martin, Joseph W. 'The Pre-Quaker Writings of George Bishop,' *Quaker History* 74 No. 2 (Fall 1985): 20-27.

McGrath, Patrick. *Bristol and the Civil War.* Bristol: Bristol Branch of the Historical Association, 1981.

—— ed. *Merchants and Merchandise in Seventeenth-Cenutry Bristol.* Bristol: Bristol Record Society.

McGregor, J.F. and Barry Reay. *Radical Religion in the English Revolution.* London: Oxford University Press, 1984.

McLachlan, John H. *Socinianism in Seventeenth-Century England.* Oxford: Oxford University Press, 1951.

Morrill, J.S. *The Revolt of the Provinces.* London: George Allen and Unwin Ltd., 1976.

Mortimer, Russell, S. 'Bristol Quaker Merchants: Some New Seventeenth Century Evidence,' *The Journal of Friends' Historical Society* 45 No. 2 (1953): 81-91.

—— *Early Bristol Quakerism: The Society of Friends in the City 1654-1700.* Bristol: The Historical Association, 1967.

Morton, A.L. *The World of the Ranters.* London and Southampton: The Camelot Press, Ltd., 1970.

O'Malley, T.P. 'The Press and Quakerism 1653-1659,' *The Journal of Friends' Historical Society.* 54 No. 4 (1979).

Owen, G.D., 'The Conspiracy of Christopher Love,' *Transactions of the Honorable Society of Cymmrodorions,* 1964.

Parry, R.H. *The English Civil War and After 1642-1658.* Berkeley: University of California Press, 1970.

Pearl, V. 'The Royal Independents in the English Civil War,' *Transactions of the Royal Historical Society,* 5th series xviii (1968): 69-96.

Penney, Norman. *Extracts from State Papers Relating to Friends, 1654-1672.* London: Headley Brothers, 1913.

Philips, C.E. *Cromwell's Captains.* Freeport: Books for Libraries Press, 1938.

Plomer, H.R. *A Dictionary of the Booksellers and Printers Who Were at Work in England, Scotland and Ireland from 1641-1667.* London: Printed for the Bibliographical Society, 1907.

Potter, Lois. *Secret Rites and Secret Writings: Royalist Literature, 1641-1660.* Cambridge: Cambridge Univrsity Press, 1989.

Prall, Stuart E. *The Agitation for Law Reform during the Puritan Revolution 1640-1660.* The Hague: Martinus Nijhoff, 1966.

Raab, Felix. *The English Face of Machiavelli: A Changing Interpretation 1500-1700.* London: Routledge and Kegan Paul, 1965.

Ramsay, Robert W. *Henry Ireton.* London: Longmans, Green and Co., 1949.

Reay, Barry, 'The Authorities and Early Restoration Quakerism,' *Journal of Ecclesiastical History 34,* No. 1 (Jan. 1983): 69-84.

────── *Popular Culture in Seventeenth Century England.* New York: St. Martin's Press, 1985.

────── 'Popular Hostility Towards Quakers in Mid-*Seventeenth-Century England,*' *Social History, 5, (October 1980).*

────── *Radical Religion in the English Revolution.* Oxford, Oxford University Press, 1984.

────── *The Quakers and the English Revolution.* New York: St. Martin's Press, 1985.

Robinson, Richard. *Sieges of Bristol During the Civil War.* Bristol: Leech and Taylor, 1968.

Roger, P.G. *The Fifth Monarchy Men.* London: Oxford University Press, 1966.

Russell, Conrad. *The Origins of the English Civil War.* New York: Harper and Row, 1973.

Sacks, David H. 'The Corporate Town and the English State: Bristol's 'Little Businesses' 1625-1641,' *Past and Present* 110 (February 1986): 69-105.

────── *The Widening Gate: Bristol and the Atlantic Economy 1450-1700.* Berkeley: University of California, 1991.

Schenk, W. *The Concern for Social Justice in the Puritan Revolution.* London: Longmans Green and Co., 1948.

Shipsides, Frank and Robert Wall. *Bristol: A Maritime City.* Bristol: Redcliff Press, Ltd., 1981.

Smith, Nigel. *Literature and Revolution in England 1640-1660.* New Haven: Yale University Press, 1994.

Solt, Leo. *Saints in Arms: Puritanism and Democracy in Cromwell's Army.* Stanford: Stanford University Press, 1959.

Spalding, Ruth. *The Improbable Puritan: A Life of Bulstrode Whitelocke 1605-1675.* London: Faber and Faber, 1971.

Strauss, Leo. *Persecution and the Art of Writing.* Glencoe, IL: The Free Press, 1952.

Taft, Barbara. 'The Humble Petition of Several Colonels of the Army: Causes, Character, and Results of Military Opposition to Cromwell's Protectorate,' *Huntington Library Quarterly* No. 1 (Winter 1978).

Thomas, Keith. *Religion and the Decline of Magic*. New York: Scribner, 1971.

Underdown, David. *Revel, Riot and Rebellion: Popular Politics and Culture in England 1603-1660*. Oxford: Oxford University Press, 1985.

—— *Royalist Conspiracy in England 1659-1660*. New Haven: Yale University Press, 1960.

—— *Somerset in the Civil War and Interregnum*. London: David and Charles: Newton Abbott, 1973.

—— 'The Chalk and the Cheese: Contrasts Among English Clubmen,' *Past and Present* 85 (November 1979).

—— 'Independents and Revolutionaries,' *Journal of British Studies*. vii (1968): 11-31.

—— 'The Independents Again,' *The Journal of British Studies*. VIII No. 1 (November 1968): 83-93.

—— 'The Independents Reconsidered,' *Journal of British Studies*, 3 (1964): 57-84.

Vanes, Jean. *Education and Apprenticeship in Sixteenth Century Bristol*. Bristol: The Bristol Branch of the Historical Association, 1982.

Vann, Richard T. 'The Social Origins of the Early Quakers,' *Past and Present* 48 (1970): 156-164.

—— *The Social Development of English Quakerism 1655-1755*. Cambridge, MA: Harvard University Press, 1969.

—— 'Quakerism and the Social Structure in the Interregnum,' *Past and Present* 43 (1969): 72-91.

Venn, J.A. and John Venn comps. *The Book of Matriculation and Degrees: A Catalogue of Those Who Have Been Matriculated or Been Admitted to Any Degree in the University of Cambridge from 1544-1659*. Cambridge: Cambridge University Press, 1913.

Walzer, Michael. *The Revolution of the Saints: A Study in the Origins of Radical Politics*. New York: Atheneum, 1969.

Wedgwood, C.V. *The King's Peace 1637-1641*. New York: MacMillian, 1969.

—— *The King's War 1641-1647*. New York: MacMillan, 1959.

—— *A Coffin for King Charles*. New York: MacMillan, 1964.

Wing, Donald. *Short-Title Catalogue of Books Printed in England, Scotland, Ireland, Wales and British America and of English Books Printed in Other Countries*

1641-1700. 2 vols. New York: The Modern Language Association of America, 1972.

Woodhouse, A.S.P., ed., *Puritanism and Liberty, Being the Army Debates (1647-1649) from the Clarke Manuscripts with Supplementary Documents.* London: J.M. Dent and Sons Ltd., 1950.

Woolf, Don M. *Milton and the Puritan Revolution.* New York: Humanities Press, 1963.

Woolrich, A.P. *Printing in Bristol.* Bristol: The Historical Assocation, 1985.

Woolrych, Austin. 'The Calling of Barebone's Parliament,' *English Historical Review* LXXX (1965): 492-513.

—— *Commomwealth to Protectorate.* Oxford: Oxford University Press, 1982.

—— *England Without a King 1649-1660.* London and New York: Methuen, 1983,

—— 'The Good Old Cause and the Fall of the Protectorate,' *Cambridge Historical Journal* XIII No. 1 (1957): 133-161.

—— *Penruddock's Rising, 1655.* London: The Historical Association, 1955.

—— *Soldiers and Statesmen: The General Counsel of the Army and its Debates, 1647-1648.* Oxford: Clarendon Press, 1987.

—— *The Battles of the English Civil War.* London: Batsford, 1961.

Worden, Blair. 'Persecution and Toleration,' *Papers Read at the Twenty-Second Summer Meeting and the Twenty-Third Winter Meeting of the Ecclesiastical History Society.* London: Basil Blackwell, 1984, 199-233.

—— 'Providence and Politics in Cromwellian England,' *Past and Present.* 109 (1985): 55-99.

—— *The Rump Parliament 1648-1653.* Cambridge: Cambridge University Press, 1974.

Wrightson, Keith. *English Society 1580-1680.* London: Hutchinson and Co. Pub. Ltd., 1982.

Yule, G. *The Independents in the English Civil War.* Cambridge: Cambridge University Press, 1958.

—— 'Independents and Revolutionaries,' *The Journal of British Studies* VII No. 2 (May 1968): 11-32.

Zagorin, Perez. *A History of Political Thought in the English Revolution.* London: Routledge and Kegan Paul, 1954.

UNPUBLISHED THESES

Cole, W.A. 'The Quakers and Politics, 1652-1660,' Ph.D. Dissertation, Cambridge University, 1955.

Goertz, Robert K. 'To Plant the Pleasant Fruit Tree of Freedom: Consciousness, Politics, and Community in Digger and Early Quaker Thought,' Ph.D. Dissertation, City University of New York Graduate Center, 1977.

Hall, D.J. 'An Historical Study of the Discipline of the Society of Friends 1738-1861,' M.A. Thesis, Durham University, 1972.

Mortimer, Russell S. 'Quakerism in Seventeenth Century Bristol,' M.A. Thesis, University of Bristol, 1946.

INDEX

Bishop, Thomas, 9

Blasphemy Act of 1648, 5

Booth, George, 102-3

Boteler, Major General William, 71-73

Bradshaw, John, 30-31, 38, 58, 61, 62, 73

Bristol,
army in protects Quakers, 59-60, 68, 72
city politics, 54-55
civil war in, 14-15
effect of civil war on, 14-16, 26, 27-28, 54-55, 78
political discontent before civil wars, 12-14
reaction to Quakers, 60-61, 64-69, 71-72, 104
riots in, 67-68, 104

Burroughs, Edward, 61

CAMM, JOHN, 59, 67-69

Canne family, 10-11

Canne, William, 10-11, 67

Cavendish, William, Marquis of Newcastle, 32-33, 40

Charles I, 13, 20

Civil War,
Battle of Naseby, 16-17
Battle of Worcester, 45-46

Clarendon, Henry Hyde, Earl of, 102

Coke, Thomas, 40, 41

Committee for Discoveries and Examinations, 29

Council of State, 23, 24, 27, 29-30, 38, 46-47, 51-53, 55-56, 76, 96-97

Craven, William, Lord, 30, 32-37

Cromwell, Oliver,
on religious toleration, 49-50, 77-78, 80-81, 91, 96
reacts to Quakers, 77-78

FALCONER, MAJOR RICHARD, 32-33, 34, 36-37

Farmer, Ralph, 37-45, 55, 56, 67, 74, 92-95

Fell, Judge Thomas, 82

Fell, Margaret, 58, 69, 82-83

First Dutch War, 47-48, 51

Fleetwood, Major General Charles, 18-19, 26, 30, 45-46, 98, 101, 102

Forest of Dean, 23-24

Fox, George,
as Quaker organizer, 58
in contact with Bishop, 79-82, 84
jailed, 79-81
Journal of, 58

GLYNN, CHIEF JUSTICE JOHN, 80-81

Gouldney, Thomas, 63, 102

HAGGETT, JUDGE JOHN, 27, 56-57

Harrison, Major General THOMAS, 23, 30, 38, 45, 50, 53, 55, 61, 62, 107

Hollister, Dennis, 55, 56, 60-61, 63, 71-72, 102, 107

Howgill, Francis, 61

Humble Petition and Advice, 94, 101

INDEPENDENTS, 1-5, 22, 41, 59

Instrument of Government, 56-57, 64, 80, 89-90, 94

Ireton, Commissary General Henry, 5

LAMBERT, MAJOR GENERAL JOHN, 30, 45, 50, 102, 103

Launceton gaol, 79